'An invaluable resource from two seasoned pro[ ]
the skills and the practice needed for voiceo[ ]
other voiceover professionals, from agents to [ ]
useful. Chapters on how to prepare a voice reel, how to work with different styles
of voiceover script, what to expect in a studio and how to comport yourself as a
voiceover professional are an absolute must for any student or actor interested in
developing this aspect of their work. And the practical summaries and glossary make
the book even better!'
Judith Phillips, Head of Voice at LAMDA

'I feel cheated. Over 30 years in the business I have steadily built up an arsenal of
knowledge, understanding, techniques, exercises, hints, tips and secrets, which I call
on daily in my role as a voiceover artist. And now here it all is in 115 pages!
This is a practical, sensible guide that will equip aspiring artists with the essential tools
and know-how to help build a career in voiceovers.'
Ben Fairman, Managing Director, Radioville and Voiceover Artist

'Stephen and David explore every aspect of learning the art of 'voiceover'. It is an
essential read for the aspiring voiceover artist and would also serve as a useful frame
of reference for the more seasoned professional too!
This is an excellent read, both in terms of plain English 'textbook' advice and practical
step-by-step guide to learning and succeeding in voiceover. Stephen and David
impart years of experience in a concise and humorous way that only seasoned
veterans can. Learning the ropes of 'voiceover' can literally take years. Stephen and
David clearly set out a framework to help the aspiring artist and give them the very
best chance of success.'
Max McGonigal, Crow TV

'A useful guide for prospective new voice artists, and for existing artists looking to
break in to new VO sectors. Helpful tips on how the industry works, from soup to nuts!'
Johnny Garcia, Rhubarb Voices

'The authors, Stephen Kemble and David Hodge, have made use of their extensive
industry experience to create the quintessential insiders' guide to voiceovers. It should
become compulsory reading at all drama schools!'
Maxine Wiltshire, Voice Shop

David Hodge
Stephen Kemble

the
VOICEOVER BOOK
DON'T EAT TOAST

Foreword by Miriam Margolyes

Illustrations by Shiv Grewal

OBERON BOOKS
LONDON

WWW.OBERONBOOKS.COM

First published in 2014 by Oberon Books Ltd
521 Caledonian Road, London N7 9RH
Tel: +44 (0) 20 7607 3637 / Fax: +44 (0) 20 7607 3629
e-mail: info@oberonbooks.com
www.oberonbooks.com

A catalogue record for this book is available from the
British Library.

PB ISBN: 978-1-78319-054-6
E ISBN: 978-1-78319-553-4

Cover design by Shiv Grewal

Illustrations copyright © Shiv Grewal

Printed, bound and converted
by CPI Group (UK) Ltd, Croydon, CR0 4YY.

Visit www.oberonbooks.com to read more about all our
books and to buy them. You will also find features, author
interviews and news of any author events, and you can
sign up for e-newsletters so that you're always first to hear
about our new releases.

For Hattie,
Laura and Sam

and everyone who has ever asked us
'How do you become a voiceover?'

The voice is one of the most powerful instruments, lying at the heart of the communications process.

Anne Karpf, *The Human Voice: The Story of a Remarkable Talent*

CONTENTS

About the Authors & Illustrator   ix

Don't Eat Toast!   xi

Foreword by Miriam Margolyes   xii

Introduction   1

PART ONE: THE VOICE   **4**

The Impact of the Voice   6

Get to Know Your Voice   7

PART TWO: THE SKILLS   **14**

Vocal Energy   16

Being in the Moment   17

Sight-Reading   18

Acting   18

Listening   19

A Sense of Timing   22

Words on a Page   24

Commercials   25

Narration   30

Animation   32

Audiobooks   42

Other Work   44

PART THREE: THE STUDIO   **46**

Technicalities   48

Before the Session   53

The Session   55

PART FOUR: THE BUSINESS   62

Knowing your Strengths   64
Showreels   66
Getting Work   73
Finding an Agent   74

PART FIVE: VOICE AND BODY   78

Posture and Breath   80
A Vocal Warm-Up   84
Looking After Your Voice   89
Dyslexia   90

AND ...   92

Other Crumbs of Advice   94
In a Nutshell ...   101
Terminology   102
Further Reading   106
Our Thanks ...   107
Audio/Visual Resource Pack File Listing   109
Notes   111

ABOUT THE AUTHORS & ILLUSTRATOR

DAVID HODGE

David's career began as a sound engineer at the outset of commercial radio in the UK. He recorded many voiceovers for radio and TV commercials, as well as documentaries, animation series, corporate programmes, audiobooks, foreign language versions and the like. During this time he made one of the first professional voiceover showreels. His reputation for this aspect of work grew and he was much in demand by many high-profile voices of the time.

During his fifteen years as a sound engineer he became a founding Director and shareholder of Silk Sound studios in London where he also produced and directed a number of award-winning radio commercials.

Moving away from engineering he spent six years as Studio Manager for Saunders & Gordon, another successful audio post-production facility. A two-year period of freelance followed with much of the time spent as voice director on *Maisy*, a BAFTA award-winning animation series for the under-fives.

For twelve years he was heavily involved in the running of Hobsons International, a prominent voiceover and artists' agency. He regularly gave talks at accredited drama schools and developed The Hobsons Prize, an annual award for graduating drama students.

He continues to give talks, workshops and also offers a bespoke showreel service.

STEPHEN KEMBLE

Stephen comes from an acting background including extensive work as a voiceover. He has worked across a broad range of media; commercial campaigns, narration for documentary programmes and current affairs series, corporate work, TV promotions and audiobooks.

In 2006 he graduated with distinction from the MA Voice Studies course at The Royal Central School of Speech and Drama. Since then he has worked with actors in production, teaching 'practical voice' to actors in training and developing his teaching of voice for microphone. In 2011 he became a designated Linklater teacher.

He has devised and run voiceover technique workshops for MA Voice Studies students at The Royal Central School of Speech and Drama and also for graduating students at the Bristol Old Vic Theatre School, London Academy of Music and Dramatic Art and the Royal Welsh College of Music and Drama.

For several years he has worked as a text and voice coach at the Royal Shakespeare Company and is Consultant Voice Coach at the Birmingham REP.

SHIV GREWAL

Shiv has drawn since he was four years old.

And performed since he was seven.

He trained as an architect, and has been acting professionally for twenty-eight years. He is versed in traditional and digital media, including animation. He has worked as a caricaturist from Covent Garden to Richard Branson's parties.

His voiceover work includes over forty dramas for BBC Radio in London, Manchester, Birmingham and Glasgow, including *Book of the Week*, *Book at Bedtime*, and *The Archers*. He was subsequently invited to join the BBC Radio Drama Company. He has been a regular in *Westway* for BBC World Service and also for *Silver Street*.

Shiv has enjoyed voicing characters for animation including the BBC TV series *World Faiths* for Right Angle. And by a stroke of fortune he was a voiceover artist for the dance company DV8 in *Can We Talk About This*.

Highlights of Shiv's acting career include a rich relationship with Tamasha Theatre Co. as well as playing Sir Toby Belch in the West End production of *Twelfth Night*, Don Pedro at Stratford in the RSC production of *Much Ado About Nothing*, and George Khan in *East Is East* at Oldham Coliseum, amongst many others. His film work includes *Brothers In Trouble*, *My Son The Fanatic*, and *The Vanguard*.

Shiv illustrates, designs and paints, and amongst many others is inspired by the illustrator Moebius. As well as private painting commissions this year, he is in the early stages of writing and drawing a graphic novel.

DON'T EAT TOAST!

At the end of an interview with Max McGonigal, Managing Director of Crow TV, Stephen asked for his one piece of advice. 'Don't eat toast' came the response.

Stephen's look of disbelief prompted Max to explain that in a session he was directing the voiceover arrived, settled himself in the voice booth and promptly ate two slices of toast!

The inevitable lip smacking and mouth noises affected the whole session.

FOREWORD by Miriam Margolyes

How I wish this book had been available to me when I started my voiceover career in 1974.

I came from the sheltered milieu of the BBC Drama Repertory Company, playing everything from little old ladies to small boys. Then I found that the business of advertising and the world of artistic creation collided in the making of a voiceover.

It was a gentler world then and 'received pronunciation', which was my natural speech, was much in demand. Today, the voiceover must have a modern sound; perfect diction is not necessarily needed. As we all know, even Her Majesty the Queen's voice has altered, reflecting the drive towards vocal democracy.

The important thing to realise is that not everyone who has a good voice can be a voiceover. Ability to sight-read is essential, microphone position is crucial, flexibility is paramount, as is the need to understand the client. There must be a discipline and a technical ability, coupled with a keen sense of timing.

Most commercials last for thirty seconds so you have to get the message across in that time. You learn how to be fast without gabbling; you learn that emotion (which is essential for selling!) takes time and that it is the consonants that carry the sense and vowels the emotion. A common fault is losing energy at the end of the sentence, so that final words peter out indistinctly and lose their bite. The voice may be powerful and sensuous, but if it dwindles, it's useless.

I always relish being asked to create a voice for a character that can range from a housewife to a carrot. I urge you to remember that there is no such thing as a 'voice.' There can only be a PERSON, so whatever the words might be in the script, I always ask 'what is the age and class of the carrot?' because that will help me to create the person from whom the voice comes. When you record, see in your mind who you are, what kind of mood the character is in and use all that knowledge in the sound you make. There can be huge satisfaction in getting it right, and when you hear the playback (and you must ALWAYS ask to hear it) you know you've created something perfect and complete.

When I began, it was common to be in a studio with lots of other actors; it was fun and sometimes raucous. Now we live in a pared-down world and it's a rare treat to work with colleagues across the mic. There is more and more competition, lower wages, a tougher working environment and smaller budgets. But I have to say... it's still fun.

And your attitude can make it fun; the client will appreciate a sunny personality, so whatever your real mood might be, when you walk into the studio, bring happiness with you.

Good luck!

Has anyone ever said that you've an ...
interesting ... wonderful voice ..?

Have you ever heard a voiceover and
thought, 'I could do that'?

Have you thought of becoming a voiceover
... and wondered what it's all about?

Are you an actor looking to develop
the scope of your working life?

INTRODUCTION

A voiceover is a professional performer putting their voice and skills up for hire in a sophisticated multi-media world.

They're employed to bring the words of a particular script to life; to inform, guide or persuade by attracting the audience with their vocal quality and performance.

We've often been asked 'How do you become a voiceover?', 'What is it you need to do?'

When we explain that it's a craft requiring many skills, we're often met with a look of puzzlement. It's a frequent misconception that, because we all have a voice and use it on a daily basis, 'Surely *anyone* can be a voiceover?'

Well not quite.

> *'Someone's told me I've got a good voice.'*
> *That alone though doesn't qualify you to be a voiceover.*
>
> **Kate Davie – Voice Agent**

At the end of our seminars and workshops people frequently tell us how surprised they are to find that voiceover work is more complex than they'd thought, particularly when they grasp just how many plates you have to keep spinning in order to give a great performance.

But let's face it, whether it's plastering a wall, cooking the perfect soufflé or playing a musical instrument, the professionals we admire always manage to make their particular skill look effortless. What we rarely see, and frequently forget, is the time and energy spent in endless practice to reach that standard of performance.

You'll hear voiceovers in many different situations; commercials, documentaries, animation films, public transport, lifts, satnav systems, websites, phone menus, audiobooks and more.

In writing this book we want to recognise voiceover as a craft and unravel some of the myths and mysteries of this fascinating and potentially rewarding job.

If then, prompted by comments from friends, colleagues or even your own 'inner' voice, you're curious about this work, we will help you discover your potential, explain what's involved and give you the essential information you'll need to get started. We have also included some useful opinions and advice from a number of professionals involved in various aspects of the industry.

We know from experience that when someone is considering work as a voiceover, the first thing they often do is make a showreel. Without some basic knowledge of what is expected and the skills involved, this can be a costly mistake and lead to a string of rejections by agents.

Our aim then is to prepare you to succeed in what is a very competitive market.

The book has five key sections.

In **Part One** we look at the importance of becoming familiar with your own voice and significantly, the way others hear you. **Part Two** looks at the skills involved and how they are applied to the various areas of the industry.

Every recording session will be a different experience, so **Part Three** will give you an idea of what to expect in a studio and also explain some of the technical aspects that involve you. In **Part Four** we bring all this together with a look at the business of being a voiceover and how to get started. Your body has a major influence on how you sound, so **Part Five** considers the physical aspects of being a voiceover.

Finally, in **And ...** there's more advice from the industry experts, key points from the book, a list of terminology and a few suggestions for further reading.

David and Stephen

PART ONE
THE VOICE

So that's what I sound like!

PART ONE – THE VOICE

It's important to know your voice; its range and its limits.

The Impact of the Voice

The VOICE plays a vital role in the way we express ourselves. In a predominantly visual world, surrounded by numerous images, it's easy to overlook just how central it is in our day-to-day interactions with each other. Consider how easy it is to misinterpret the *tone* of a text message or an email. But, if the message is spoken, then the meaning is likely to be less ambiguous.

A voice can be revealing in so many subtle ways. If you *listen* carefully to a speech-based programme on the radio, a podcast, the news or an audiobook, you soon realise just how important the *expressive* quality of the voice is in communicating thoughts and emotions.

The voice has the power to connect with us on a very deep level and can also reveal much about us as a person – gender, birthplace, personality. It can be aggressive, seductive, harsh, soothing, and in these qualities, show confidence, power, affection, weakness. Furthermore, the subtleties of speech can be manipulated to translate emotions; persuade, cajole, inform, irritate, reprimand. The way we speak is a vital part of how we present ourselves to the world. Whether consciously or subconsciously, we often manipulate our voice to make it fit the image we want to project, or the various situations in which we find ourselves. How many of us, for example, have a phone voice?

Get to Know Your Voice

Despite the many similarities between those of us that share the same language or accent, our own voice is unique.

Using Voice Biometrics, a sophisticated system of recording and analysis, even identical twins can be told apart.

An essential element of being a voiceover is understanding your voice; getting to know the qualities and potential; to realise why *your* voice might be chosen over another and what it is that makes you different, albeit not to the degree of a biometric voiceprint!

Being familiar with your voice is particularly important when you're starting out and need to convince a voice agent how unique you are.

To achieve this you'll need to explore your voice in detail and specifically the way others hear it. This will help you understand its range and importantly, begin to reveal what style of voice work will suit you. You may also discover qualities you didn't think you had and therefore expand your potential.

By *listening* carefully to your voice you can also learn to be more objective about it, which in time will improve your performance as a voiceover.

So why does your voice sound the way it does? Why don't we all sound the same?

Bone structure, the formation of the vocal folds and resonating spaces above them are unique to each of us and account for our particular sound. It's the vocal equivalent of a fingerprint and makes us recognisable to those who know us.

External factors also play a part. There will have been many, many influences throughout your life that contribute to the way you sound today. Home life is often very influential. If you came from a large family for example, you may have had to raise your voice to be heard. Peers in your social circle at school, college or work will also have had an effect, as will factors such as: ill health, corrective dental work, a chewing gum habit, smoking, surgery, actor voice-training, singing in a band, frequently moving home as a child and the programmes you watched on TV. These are just a few examples, the variations are almost limitless.

Give some thought to this and write your own list. In workshops we encourage people to draw pictures or make a collage to help give these influences a reality.

The sum of the person you are informs the way you sound or speak.

Christopher Kent – Producer

Accent

The sound you make is shaped into speech by the lips, jaw, tongue and its action on other parts of the mouth. One of the outstanding characteristics of your speech will be your accent. The geography, climate or culture of the place or places in which you grew up will have contributed to this.

Some people consider their accent to be an obstacle to becoming a voiceover. But there's no reason not to use your native accent; on the contrary, it's to be encouraged.

> I'd never use someone from the South who says 'I can do a really good Geordie accent', I'd use someone who's from Newcastle.
>
> **Ben Fairman – Producer**

Regional accents are now widely accepted. That said, very 'thick' accents may have a limited appeal simply because they may not be easily grasped by a wider audience.

RP or 'neutral' accents are often specifically requested by clients; what they're hoping for is something that's clear and intelligible. This is often a factor if a commercial is scheduled to be broadcast across the network.

A standard, southern-English RP (Received Pronunciation) accent, in the past often described as 'BBC English', is often thought of as being 'posh'. These days when producers ask for RP they generally mean a much more relaxed version, which may even contain hints of an accent.

Having something that is considered a standard accent is not unique to the UK. In America, for example, their equivalent is known as 'General American (GE)' or 'Standard American English (SAE)'. It's become their accepted neutral for voiceover work, particularly in news presenting.

Meanwhile, regional accents have been gaining popularity. Over the years there have been various surveys carried out on behalf of advertisers to determine which accents are more favourable for commercials. Some years ago, for example, Scottish accents were perceived as being trustworthy and as a consequence were often used in campaigns for the financial sector.

These preferences tend to come and go and further research has revealed that it's the quality of voice, how the listener is spoken to, that matters more than the accent.

> I get offended by people saying that some accents are _more_ friendly – no they're not. They're not _less_ friendly either, it's the attitude behind the accent that makes the difference.
>
> **Paul Burke – Producer**

So, as far as *your* accent is concerned, you can decide to:

• Develop your natural voice and trust that it'll be popular in the wider market place.

• Learn to modify your accent towards a more neutral position so that you can offer an alternative when required.

A voiceover is employed to sell or inform by attracting the audience, and while accent and age may be important factors, there's no doubt it's the *sound* that will make the greatest initial impact. Some voices of course, are instantly appealing, some are an acquired taste, while others simply grate. But, the appeal of a voice is entirely subjective.

> We're always looking for texture and something that's not bland. Something that has an edge to it or a recognisable factor or ... just an interesting voice!
>
> **Martin Sims – Producer**

The sudden rise in popularity of an accent or voice, specifically in advertising, is often influenced by the latest popular TV series – clients are frequently inspired by what they see and hear around them.

What is always important however, irrespective of accent or vocal quality, is connecting with your audience and being understood.

The Way Others Hear You

How would you describe your voice?

To prompt you, here are a few popular adjectives used to describe the quality of voices. Circle those which apply to you. There'll be more than one and, of course, you can add any of your own that you feel are relevant.

Assured	Engaging	Quirky
Animated	Enthusiastic	Reassuring
Authoritative	Erudite	Rich
Believable	Fresh	Sassy
Bright	Friendly	Scary
Bubbly	Funny	Scatty
Camp	Geeky	Self-Assured
Charming	Gentle	Sensitive
Chatty	Gravelly	Smooth
Cheeky	Happy	Soft
Chocolaty	Hard	Soothing
Clipped	Hip	Sophisticated
Compelling	Husky	Street
Contemporary	Irritating	Suave
Cool	Laddish	Sultry
Cultured	Light	Tough
Cute	Mature	Upbeat
Deep	Mellow	Vibrant
Distinctive	No-Nonsense	Warm
Downbeat	Parental	Whiny
Dry	Posh	
Elegant	Powerful	
Energetic	Precise	

When you speak, not only do you *hear* your voice on the airborne sound-waves, but you also *feel* it as it resonates through your bones. To give you some idea, put your hand on your upper chest or the bones of your face and speak aloud. Can you feel the vibrations?

No one else *hears* your voice in this way, they only hear the airborne sound-waves.

It's important therefore, that you become familiar with the way others hear you, because ultimately that's what you're selling as a voiceover.

Getting to know your voice in this way will also help you become more objective, which will inevitably improve your performance.

How Can I Hear My Own Voice?

To begin this exploration take a moment to look in a mirror – really LOOk.

Is one eye bigger than the other? Does your nose point slightly left or right, does your mouth tend to curl up or down at the corners? These shouldn't be judgements, just observations.

This is *exactly* the kind of detailed attention that you need to pay to your voice.

To begin, hold your hands out *flat* and cup your ears. Now speak as you would normally. Keep speaking and take your hands away. Notice the difference? This crude exercise will give you a very basic idea of how someone else hears you.

To improve this exercise, use what we refer to as 'The Audio Mirror'!

This simply means recording and then carefully *listening* back to yourself. Most computers or smartphones have some kind of recording software. They won't produce a high-quality, professional recording, but the recording will give you a reasonable experience of hearing your voice.

 Invest in a USB microphone, some speakers and a simple recording programme for your computer; Audacity for PC works well and MACs have Garage Band as standard.

What should you record? Start by telling a simple story or incident from your life. Imagine telling it to a good friend, in a relaxed and casual way.

When you've finished, *listen* back and note the 'natural' way you speak in this situation. It may surprise you to know that much of the time as a voiceover you'll be expected to deliver scripts in this one-to-one, conversational style, albeit with the *vocal energy* demanded by the project.

Now, *listen* again to the recording you've just made and this time consider – does your voice sound the way you thought it sounded?

Reactions to this exercise vary enormously:

> 'Surely I don't sound like that!' ...
>
> 'It's much higher than I thought' ...
>
> 'Is that a lisp?' ...
>
> 'I didn't realise I was so gruff'...
>
> 'My voice is so deep'...
>
> 'I sound so...camp!'

Or, even ...

> 'I don't *like* the sound of my voice!'

What's your *first* response?

 Be aware that your voice can reveal subtle aspects of our personality, this is why analysing it can sometimes feel uncomfortable.

Using the same list of adjectives as you did earlier, how would you now describe your voice? Compare the two lists. Are there any significant revelations? It'll help to make notes and date them so you can see how your opinions change over time.

Assured	Engaging	Quirky
Animated	Enthusiastic	Reassuring
Authoritative	Erudite	Rich
Believable	Fresh	Sassy
Bright	Friendly	Scary
Bubbly	Funny	Scatty
Camp	Geeky	Self-Assured
Charming	Gentle	Sensitive
Chatty	Gravelly	Smooth
Cheeky	Happy	Soft
Chocolaty	Hard	Soothing
Clipped	Hip	Sophisticated
Compelling	Husky	Street
Contemporary	Irritating	Suave
Cool	Laddish	Sultry
Cultured	Light	Tough
Cute	Mature	Upbeat
Deep	Mellow	Vibrant
Distinctive	No-Nonsense	Warm
Downbeat	Parental	Whiny
Dry	Posh	
Elegant	Powerful	
Energetic	Precise	

You could now repeat this exercise using some simple text from a magazine or newspaper. Compare the results. How different are they? Does this read sound more formal?

At some point it would be useful and interesting to ask friends and family what they think. Does their opinion match yours? If not, then who do you feel is the more accurate? And why? Finding out the qualities of your voice others hear, but you don't, is often surprising and enlightening.

After this careful scrutiny it's well worth creating a short description of your voice. It can be quite snappy, something like:

'Strong and controlled' or

'Firm, friendly and likeable' or

'Warm, natural, but authoritative and intelligent'

Over time, as you gain experience, you can always revise it. But when it comes to approaching a voice agent you will have a much better idea of what you're offering them.

Incidentally ... we are not suggesting that you develop a static attitude to your voice. This is how you sound *today*, a moment in time. Your voice will naturally evolve through experience, ageing and other effects. If you say 'This is the definitive description of my voice' then you may be denying yourself a world of possibilities.

In exploring the influences that have affected the way you sound and speak you'll come to realise that they're all part and parcel of 'what my voice is'. By shaking up the thinking about your voice you'll be aware that there are many possibilities and many shades of 'who you are' vocally.

So, having thought about the qualities of your voice, it's now worth considering, in the context of voiceovers, what it will do. Perhaps as importantly, what it *won't* do.

Ask yourself questions such as:

- Is my voice high or low pitched?
- Do I sound young or old?
- Do I speak clearly, quickly, quietly, confidently?
- Do I sound serious, or frivolous?

Becoming familiar with your voice and specifically the way others hear you, is fundamental. It's the foundation on which everything rests. This awareness, combined with a knowledge of essential vocal skills, will help you understand what your strengths are as a potential voiceover, something we'll look at more closely in **Part Four**.

Now let's consider the skills involved ...

PART TWO
THE SKILLS

PART TWO – THE SKILLS

It's one thing being familiar with your voice, but understanding and acquiring the skills of a voiceover will help you use it effectively.

Being able to work in the style of the writing, connect to the words, sound authentic and convincing, take direction and attract the listener with a performance is the job of a voiceover. All this without the subtle support of facial expression and body language that we take for granted when we have visual contact with a speaker.

How do you recognise when someone has these skills? Can you tell a good performance from a mediocre one? What is it that makes the difference?

Vocal Energy

For a moment think back to a time when you were listening to someone speaking and your attention drifted almost immediately. Chances are it wasn't *what* was being said, but *how* it was being said; perhaps the words just sounded lifeless and dull?

 If this was your experience then very likely it lacked a key ingredient, **vocal energy**, and we all instinctively know when we *don't* hear it.

It's useful to develop 'vocal awareness'. You can do this by *listening* **to a variety of voices, in all sorts of situations, and as you do, consider the immediate impact a particular voice has on you. Does it attract or repel? What effect does it have on you and why?**

Participants in our workshops have often defined it in terms of volume and/or speed, but this isn't it. If you've ever heard a great storyteller who kept you really involved in the tale and wanting to hear more, the chances are it was their vocal energy that engaged you.

It's easy to take for granted the complex activity that begins with absorbing the thoughts from the page and ends with the spoken word. It requires freedom in breath, sound and speech and includes variations in pace and pitch, and the use of pause and emphasis.

These are the elements often used to technically describe the concept of vocal energy. In the best circumstances, however, this chain of events is instinctive and vocal energy is part of the transformation that occurs when the speaker embodies the intention of the writer and provokes the effect the writer means to have on the listener.

> *You've got to really mean it, you've got to really feel it …*
> *and just want to communicate.*
>
> **Elizabeth Conboy — Voiceover**

Common substitutes for vocal energy include over-loud delivery, unnaturally emphatic speech and artificial variations in pitch.

Being in the Moment

What did I just say?

Being mindfully aware of what's going on right here and now, with no other distracting thoughts, is key. Many performers describe the moment when they're on stage, on the field of play in the studio, on set, when the earth just seems to fall away and they're truly connected with what they are doing.

If you're not in the moment, it's perfectly possible to read the words on the page, let them go into your brain and out of your mouth without any connection with what you're saying.

When you're connected with what the script is trying to say, you will breathe life into the written word in a natural and engaging way. You can practise being in the moment in everyday situations such as having a cup of coffee.

Sight-Reading

Sight-reading (sometimes referred to as cold-reading) is to communicate a piece of text which you are seeing for the first time with accuracy, clarity and the appropriate intention and mood.

Generally there's no rehearsal time when recording commercials and typically you'll not see the script in advance. Given that you must be able to produce a credible, confident performance within a very short time, it's essential to have good sight-reading skills.

The best way to improve is to read aloud. A few minutes of practice every day will really pay off. As you do, it might help to use a finger to direct your gaze along the lines. This will stop you from skipping down. It will also help you to follow the sentences to the full stops and prevent you from energetically ending a thought at other punctuation marks before the sense of the line is complete.

It may also help to 'chunk' the text. Use a small piece of folded paper to block out some of the words so that your eye cannot skip down.

The more you practise, the more fluent you will become and the more space you will allow for your instinctive responses to contribute to your performance.

Almost any written word will do. Challenge yourself with a wide variety of material, but read whatever it is in an appropriate manner. That is to say, a romantic story will need a different performance from a technical journal or a news item. Never whisper or mumble during this practice.

You can take this one stage further by recording and *listening* to yourself as you did earlier.

There are some specific exercises that will further improve your sight-reading skills on pp. 87-89.

> *Sight-reading is really important, particularly as you might get some jobs that are very last minute or where there might be script changes.*
>
> **Nico Lennon — Voiceover**

Acting

Many in the industry believe actors make the best voiceovers, (indeed voice work is sometimes referred to as 'voice acting'.) It's assumed that, either through training or experience, actors have the necessary skills to bring scripts to life.

Not being an actor doesn't exclude you from becoming a voiceover, we all have the ability to modify our vocal expression to suit the situation, using an intimate whisper or a shout of frustration. However, being able to summon these expressive qualities, modify them on demand to suit the script and sometimes make them 'larger than life', is where some basic acting technique will always be useful – as would an understanding of character development. There are many acting courses to be found online.

Is this a microphone I see before me?

That said, while there's no doubt acting skills are of value, there's also no guarantee that one skill *automatically* leads to the other. In reality there are some fine actors who blossom in front of a microphone while others feel very uncomfortable. Equally, there are many non-actors who make very good voiceovers.

If you're good on stage, don't necessarily think you're going to be good in a very small recording booth, with cans on and working to picture, or in an ensemble with four or five other people. There isn't an automatic correlation between being on stage and being a voiceover artist.

Tony Church – Producer

Listening

Voice work is as much about *listening* as it is about speaking.

Hearing is a sense we all have, but *listening* is a key skill.

Not just casual, but really attentive listening; understanding what is being said, without the prejudice of our own judgements distorting what we hear. It goes hand in hand with 'being in the moment'; you cannot allow yourself to be distracted by what else is going on around you. The need to *listen* effectively is crucial and crops up time and again as a voiceover.

In order to deliver a script, for example, you have to *listen* objectively to the direction being given and not be side-tracked by taking what's being said as personal criticism.

You also need to *listen* to yourself carefully *and* accurately during playback in a session, so you clearly understand any adjustments that may be required.

Active *listening*, is effective *listening*. It will help you with the most important part of your job ... asking your audience to *listen* to you!

> Although you're being paid to talk ... the most important thing
> to do is listen.

Dave Peacock – Voice Director/Engineer

We've already suggested you *listen* in a focused way to your own voice. Now we want to encourage you to 'tune-in' to the world of voiceovers. Make a conscious effort to *listen* to a broad range of media output; commercial breaks, trailers, documentaries, current affairs, reality programmes and audiobooks.

As you do, consider:

- How the words are 'working' to deliver the message.
- Is there a specific emotional quality being used?
- What are the images contained within the piece? (picture them in your mind if they're not on a screen)
- What about the pace?
- Is it informing, selling, inviting ... ?

By doing this you will sharpen your *listening* skills and begon to appreciate how voices interact with the product or programme; you'll become familiar with the variety of 'read' styles.

Ask yourself if what you're hearing is believable.

Does it engage you?

Does it persuade you?

> There's got to be a belief in what you're selling.

Ben Fairman – Producer

You will also begin to recognise some of the conventions. For example in programme trailers, the end-line will contain information in a familiar sequence: the programme title ... the day it's on ... the time ... and the channel.

'Voiceover Skills, next Wednesday at 8, on Channel Z.'

Listen to commercial breaks and concentrate on the vocal performances. Really get behind why they might have been chosen, what they might have been asked to do, how they ended up with that style of performance, why did they emphasise that?

Nick Angell – Engineer/Voice Director

In becoming familiar with various deliveries, it's nonetheless important to remain true to yourself and bring your own individuality to a read rather than becoming a clone of any specific style.

Don't put on what you think is the voice other people want to hear. Don't do me an impression of someone doing an advertising voiceover because that won't help.

Pam Myers – Producer

You will also hear examples that won't reflect any of the things we've been talking about, such as voices that make you feel battered by the information they're giving; voices that seem to be a pastiche or voices far removed from a natural style. But you can learn as much from these examples as from good ones.

Join in

To help you get the feel for voice work, pick examples that appeal to you. As you become familiar with them, begin to speak along with the voiceover, mirroring what's being said. It doesn't have to be word perfect, but enough to absorb the rhythm, energy, pace and style.

As you do this it'll become increasingly clear;

- Which style of script suits your voice and reading style.
- Which will be fine with a little work.
- Which are just not your thing.

This is not to restrict or typecast you, as it's likely to be a fairly broad canvas, but it will help you begin to recognise your strengths.

 This will be particularly helpful when you come to make your first showreel.

It will be useful to record yourself, as you did earlier. Transcribe scripts from the internet, radio or TV (use the subtitles). As before, you can also use advertising copy from newspapers and magazines. Be as honest and discerning about your performance as you can, make changes and repeat the process until you feel you've achieved the best result. Again it would be worth asking friends for feedback about your performance.

Being objective will help you develop an awareness about your vocal performance. Just as chefs continually taste the food they're cooking and adjust the seasoning accordingly, so you should *listen* carefully to playbacks and note what was good and what you feel could be better.

Just a soupçon more emphasis I think.

Developing an 'internal director' is a valuable asset. Eventually it will help you work *with* your clients to create a great performance.

Inflections and Emphasis

It's important to have a connection with language and to be able to interpret a script in a way that lets the emphasis fall naturally and the inflections feel right. It's equally important, when taking direction, to make changes to these aspects of the delivery quickly and accurately – even if they go against your natural instincts.

This again highlights the need to sharpen up your *listening* skills.

Truly understand the sense of what you're delivering. Because emphasis, inflections, attitudes will naturally fall into place if you've really got behind what's trying to be communicated.

Nick Angell – Engineer/Voice Director

A Sense of Timing

(This section is laid out in a script format so you can practise reading text to time. You can read them individually or in various combinations.)

Commercials are made to specific lengths, typically; 10, 30, 40 and 60 seconds, because media companies sell advertising time in these units.	**10 secs**

It's useful to get a feel for the various
lengths, so that eventually you'll
develop an inner clock and have an
indication of the pace that's
needed for a particular script.
Occasionally, you may be asked to
'shave-off' half a second from your
performance, and part of your craft
is to achieve that saving, accurately
and without sounding rushed.

20 secs

It's also useful to know when you
have seconds to spare,
so you can use the extra time more
effectively.
It's a skill you can develop, with a
little practice and a stopwatch.

10 secs

Total: **40 seconds**

*Have an appreciation for the length of a read, a sense of timing, is
a fabulous thing to have.*

Pam Myers – Producer

*Mmmmm. I think this may be
longer than 30 seconds!*

At some point however, you may come across an
over-written script where the writer hasn't given enough
time for the performance needed. A solution has to be
found, either to edit the script, modify your pace, or a
combination of both.

There are other times however, when there's no option
but to speak like a runaway train to make the script fit.
The trick is to stay calm and keep connected to the
thoughts and your breath. If you admit to yourself that
you're feeling rushed, then that's how you'll sound.
Some copy of course is always read at speed. Examples
of this are the Terms & Conditions and legal disclaimers
that, by regulation, have to be included at the end
of some products. You may have heard variations of
'subject to availability, terms and conditions apply'.

Remember pace is reflected in the rhythm of how the thoughts build in the writing. This delivers the energy required of the read. Don't confuse this with sheer speed.

Achilles Heel

Throughout your working life there will probably be a phrase or word that turns out to be your *Achilles Heel* and the sight of which fills you with dread. Voiceovers come up with various ways to distract their brains at these times. Those that we've come across include a little flick of the hand or squeezing the thumb and forefinger together as you come up to the challenge.

Every single person has a word or phrase they don't like saying. Mine is 'Services of a solicitor' which I can't say without sounding pissed!

Chris Kent – Voiceover

Words on a Page

When you hold a script in your hand all you have before you is a collection of words in a particular order, to be spoken in a certain length of time. They may be well-written and you may have been given a brief as to how those words might be interpreted. But, until you start speaking them they remain just that ... words on a page.

For the most part, you'll be expected to give life to the script in a natural and engaging way. The way you achieve that will make your 'read' unique. No two voiceovers will read a script in quite the same way.

You're the only person who can do your read.

Chris Kent – Producer

Voiceovers are heard across a broad range of media.

In a visual programme, whether selling or informing, they are used to support the images. In non-visual media, such as radio or audiobooks however, the focus is entirely on the voice.

It all begins with a script and broadly there are two types; **short-form**, such as commercials and trailers for TV and cinema, and **long-form**, such as documentary and corporate narrations.

Commercials

A commercial script may feature:

- A single voice throughout.
- A voice for the main part and another for the end-line.
- Various characters and a straight voice end-line.

There's rarely a specific character description on which to base a performance. In order to bring authenticity to your read and bring the script to life, it'll help if you imagine a version of yourself that's appropriate to the script. For example, if it's a high-powered sales pitch, then you might imagine yourself as a 'really motivated salesperson'. Having something specific in your mind will keep your read style natural.

I don't think voice work is really any different from acting ... all acting is creating a person, using both the bricks of your own character and melding them with something outside yourself to construct a believable human being. So when you record, see in your mind who you are, what kind of mood the character is in and use all that knowledge in the sound you make.

Miriam Margolyes – Voiceover

Copywriters generally write for a specific target audience, but they tend to focus on a single member of that group. This is why the conversational, one-to-one approach is often required. It may help your read if you bring to mind someone who fits the profile of that audience. It's a really useful method to help communicate sincerely.

I always perform to an imaginary person. Who it is depends on the product, but I'll always imagine there's somebody there.

Sue Elliott-Nicholls – Voiceover

A 'natural' read is a very common request from clients. What they're hoping to avoid is the stereotype style of 'voiceover', which can often sound forced and inauthentic.

Sometimes though, 'natural' can seem at odds with the need to deliver the script with energy and clarity. Yet, that's exactly the combination you're aiming to achieve.

The Challenge

This then is the challenge. You are employed to read a piece of advertising copy, that may not naturally occur in everyday speech, in an unaffected yet heightened way, that sounds both authentic and believable.

The production team will have very specific ideas about the delivery they're looking for. Part of your skill is to understand what is needed to interpret their ideas.

As you work through the script you'll begin to appreciate that, although the message may be quite short, a lot of time has been spent composing it. Before you read it aloud, begin by mentally running through this check list:

- **What is the product?** You may have some idea about this even before you see the script.
- **Who is the script aimed at?** Are you meant to represent the target audience or not?
- **What is the focus of the main message?** Does it sell, inform, guide, persuade ...
- **What is the style or mood?** Hard, soft, authoritative, tough, gentle, tongue-in-cheek, warm, cool ... this will determine the vocal energy required.
- **What's the response** the script is trying to provoke?
- **Where's it set?** Think carefully about the location as this may affect your vocal energy. If, for example, it's set outside in the street, then you would need to slightly raise the level to compensate for traffic noise; we instinctively adjust our voices to suit our environment.

Once you've formed a broad picture, then consider:

- **How you're going to 'grab'** the listener's attention in the first few words.
- **What are the 'active' words** that chart the journey of the thoughts/feelings.
- **How do the thoughts build?**
- **Is there a backstory?** This is something that may have happened before the start of the script that influences what you're about to say.
- **How are you going to deliver the information?** You may need to break the whole into more manageable chunks. You'll often find the information builds step by step. Let the punctuation guide you, it'll shape the structure and indicate breath points. Remember though, a comma doesn't always indicate a pause ... it may point to where the thought shifts in energy, rhythm or direction. Equally it may just serve a grammatical purpose, such as either side of a name and therefore doesn't necessarily indicate a pause or a breath point. If you do use a comma as a small breath point, make sure that you're not breaking up the sense of the thought. Punctuation should help the meaning.

- **The rhythm of the script.** The writing style may give you opportunities to vary the rhythm or it may be determined by the music track, if there is one. You need to give the whole read a 'flow' that is appropriate to the content i.e. fast, slow, gentle, aggressive, upbeat, considered etc.

- **How to identify the words requiring emphasis.** The product name and features should be obvious, but there may be others. Look for the verbs that activate the thought; adjectives and nouns are also clues as to how the words are doing the 'work' and what type of read is required. The word 'NEW', for example, will announce the launch of the latest product or feature. This will likely require an upbeat read and 'NEW' will certainly need to be stressed.

Here are some other familiar upbeat words and phrases:

Free	Wonderful
Better than ever	Outstanding
Now even better	Introducing
Great prices	Ultimate
On sale now	Right solution
While stocks last	Find out more
Brighter	Today
Trust ...	Right
It has to be ...	Your chance to win
Hundreds	Book now

These words will give a clue as to the mood and Vocal Energy:

Velvety	Relax
Shiny	Committed
Take care	Fresh
Soft	Lots of fun
We pride ourselves	Gentle but effective
Imagine	Delicious/deliciously
Crispy	Coming soon
In life	Smooth
In the Summer/Winter ...	We're passionate

These suggest something informative:

Discover	To find your local ...
We'll send you	We urgently need
To find out more	Visit ...
To find out what this means	Help

For more information

- Are there repetitions of words or phrases? What effect do they have in putting the message across?
- Is the script personalised in places? How does this affect your delivery? 'You' and 'Yours' are often used to make scripts directly personal to the listener and 'We', implies that you're speaking for the company advertising their product.

From the First Word, to the Last ...

 Finding the right energy to begin and end a script can be difficult. Some start in such a way that adding an *unspoken* line before will help raise your energy to the correct level.

So, for example, if you had a script that began:

If you smoke around children, they smoke too ...

You could add (silently) ...

(Did you know,) If you smoke around children, they smoke too ...

This same technique can also be used at the end of a script.

As your brain is reading ahead and sees the end coming, there can be a tendency for the voice to tail off. But, just as a competitive runner knows not to slow down until they've actually crossed the finishing line, so must you maintain your vocal energy until the very last word.

In this situation add an *unspoken* lead-out line.

For example:

... The Voiceover magazine on sale now.

You could add;

... The Voiceover magazine on sale now. (Get your copy today.)

The End Line

End lines are often slogans created by advertising agencies to be used across a variety of media. They're used to sum up a commercial or simply added as a stamp of recognition. For example:

'Tesco, every little helps'

'HSBC, your local bank'

It's quite possible that you'll only be booked to read the end-line. How do you deliver it?

The text that comes before; the images, music, or the line itself will invariably give clues to the tone you should adopt. Everything we've said about reading a commercial applies, particularly the need for maintaining consistent vocal energy.

> *The most difficult area for voiceovers are end-lines. The fewer the words, the more difficult it is to impart meaning. Often when it's written and conceived it's never thought about how it'll sound when it's said, it's how it looks as a logo.*
>
> **Martin Sims — Producer**

Narration

Training videos, sales presentations, product demonstrations, educational programmes etc., are all examples of long-form scripts, but possibly the most familiar is the documentary, which can either be a single programme or part of a series and cover a wide range of topics. There are numerous other genres and formats such as factual, games and reality shows that often use the skills of a voiceover.

Whatever the topic, long-form scripts require you to adopt a style that communicates with the audience in an interesting and authentic way. The skill here is to sound informed and engaged in order to draw the viewer into the story being told.

This can be quite a challenge given some of the material you might have to read. Technical information can be very dry for example!

> *The skill you need, when you may not understand what you're talking about, is to make it <u>sound</u> like you know what you're talking about. And it's only when you're confident about working with text that you will ever be able to begin to lift a script like that off the page and make it sound like speech; like it's the most natural thing in the world to talk about niobium and stainless steel.*
>
> **David Holt — Voiceover**

If you're working 'to picture' (see pp. 51-52) then your narration is likely to be interspersed with spoken contributions from those appearing in the film (these are known as 'sync-sound' or 'inserts'.) Although this may give a stop/start feel to your read, you have to maintain a flow that sounds natural and integrated.

 At the various 'in-points' try to stay relaxed and avoid the tendency to snatch a breath, as they can often sound noisy and are difficult to edit out.

Equally the level of your voice has to be consistent, so that you avoid a 'blast' of sound on the first words of your text following an insert. There's more about breaths on pp. 83-84.

It's not unusual to be sent a narrative script ahead of time. Use this opportunity to:

- Note where you may have difficulty with any of the words or pronunciations.
- Know where your breath will come naturally with the thought structure.
- Get an idea of the pace you'll need by timing some of the sections.
- Work out where you can pause for effect.
- Look for target words which will need emphasis.

Scripts for corporate, educational or training programmes will often include terminology associated with the topic. The medical world immediately springs to mind; try saying *macrodystrophia lipomatosa*.

These type of scripts require an ability to grasp the details of the subject quickly and an aptitude for pronunciation.

It's likely the client will be on hand to help with anything unusual, but if you've accepted the booking, then it'll be expected that you've got the skills to tackle the material and sound convincing.

By the time you've finished recording the script, you will have thoroughly warmed to the subject matter, style and pace, and so you may be asked to re-record the opening few pages.

Long-form scripts often involve many hours in the studio and so your vocal and physical stamina will be tested.

 Have an early night beforehand and make sure you are well hydrated.

Tell the producer/engineer if you are too hot/too cold/in need of a quick break. They are not mind readers, so unless you say you are unhappy or uncomfortable, they won't know.

Tamsin Collinson — Producer

Animation and audiobooks are closer to voice acting, but still fall within what is generally considered as voiceover work.

Animation

Many voiceovers are keen to enter the world of animation, as sessions can be great fun and very creative, but it might surprise you to learn that, whether it's a TV series, feature film, video game or a corporate programme, it's unlike any other area of voiceover work.

A performer has to have great imagination, application, vocal dexterity, creativity, a good ear, comic timing, instant recall, active *listening*, the ability to improvise, as well as sight-reading skills and endless stamina.

Oh yes, and be prepared to leave inhibitions at the door!

> I think there's a misconception that animation is all about putting on silly voices ... it's not. The best characters are those that have got heart, humour and some kind of authenticity.
>
> **Helen Stroud — Animation Producer**

Even though you'll be part of a world where everything is larger than life, what you're trying to achieve is believability. The voice you create, however heightened, must inhabit the character on the screen and be credible within the context of the story.

> However extreme the character (I once had to play an angry pencil sharpener) and however bizarre the situation, you have to play it truthfully. You can hear an empty, hollow performance a mile off.
>
> If it's real in the world in which it lives, then it will work.
>
> **David Holt — Voiceover**

It requires a mastery of performing, so acting skills are essential. If you're not a trained actor, and this area of work appeals, then we encourage you to consider some of the short courses offered by drama schools. Learning about character development will be particularly valuable.

 Visit the Drama UK website.

Joining the cast of an animation project may begin with an invitation to a casting session. To reach this stage the production team will have listened to showreels and suggestions from voice agents and added you to their shortlist.

 Be prepared to travel to auditions and recording sessions out of town.

If you offer up a voice at a casting that's generally out of your range and difficult to sustain and the director goes for it, you'll almost certainly regret it and may end up damaging yourself.

I've learnt never to offer up anything that isn't vocally comfortable and that I couldn't keep reproducing accurately throughout the entire series.

Teresa Gallagher – Voiceover

Although generally unpaid, casting sessions are a chance to hear first-hand what the director hopes to achieve and for you to impress with your inventiveness and versatility.

You'll often be given a design and short description of the character/s ahead of the audition. So, have three or four ideas in mind, but in doing so, consider the intended audience; you don't want anything too scary if, for example, they happen to be pre-school kids.

Finding a voice to match the character is usually a collaborative process, as the director and production team will also have their ideas and preconceptions. As part of the process they will also want to hear that you can express a variety of emotions using the voice or voices you've created.

If you succeed in getting the part then you'll be given more information. Key characters often have a written profile that goes into some detail about their personality and status within the story. Smaller roles, with maybe only a few lines, will only have a short description. You might also be given specifics about the format of the show, so you can really immerse yourself in the production.

Once in the studio with the director and other members of the cast, there'll be more time to develop the character's voice. If it's a long series then it'll naturally bed down and develop as you begin to perform and interact with the other voices.

If you're new to this type of work, you may not yet have the experience needed to carry a leading role, but if the production team can see your potential, then you may be offered a secondary part. This will give you the opportunity to gain some experience and learn from the other actors.

Having seen the scripts we spend time talking about the characters. It might be two or three hours before we're ready to record on the first day and then we might go back if something develops during the session.

Leo Neilsen – Animation Producer

To give you some idea of a typical brief and just how detailed a character's profile can be, Collingwood & Co, a long-established, award-winning animation studio, have given us permission to reproduce the brief they sent out for their series *Ruff-Ruff, Tweet and Dave*.

This is a pre-school CGI animation co-produced with Sprout USA and an acquisition for CBeebies. The profile is for the character of Hatty the Hamster. Having sent the brief to voiceover agents, they subsequently received nearly 200 MP3 auditions.

> We listened to them all, then cut down to a list of 15–20 varying character types. We shortlisted six for broadcaster approval. The top four were then called in for face-to-face auditions at our studio, to see how they could hone and adapt their character reads with direction.
>
> Helen Stroud – Producer

You can see from the following example just how much detail and information you're often given to work with.

HATTY THE HAMSTER – CASTING

Hatty the Hamster is the fun hamster-host of a new animated series of fifty-two eleven-minute multiple-choice adventures for three- to four-year-olds.

Hatty is an adult. He's a mix of tour guide and game show host. He arrives in his Spin-Again/Bubble-Copter craft at the start of every episode, to take three friends, Ruff-Ruff, Tweet and Dave, off on a fun day out.

Hatty is the bridge between the three main characters, Ruff-Ruff, Tweet and Dave, and the audience at home. He talks directly to the audience – the only character to break the fourth wall – inviting them to participate in the show and call out the answers to a series of multiple-choice questions within the adventure. He is not a teacher and he mustn't be patronising.

He wears a different hat each week that is both a visual reminder of the theme of the episode, and of a key character trait, that he likes to take charge of a situation. Hatty always strives for things to be done properly and safely – without being officious or authoritarian. His three charges have their own ideas about what should happen and often scupper his best-laid plans by doing something quite different. Hatty will try to keep up with their inventiveness and go with the flow.

The characters and the audience at home must be pleased to see Hatty and enjoy his company. Warmth, humour and comic timing will be essential to the delivery of his lines. Authentic and characterful, not too cartoony, his voice will need to sit naturally against three real kids. Hatty is light, bright, funny and just a little scatterbrained. When asking questions, we should never feel like he knows all the answers, it's that he's not quite sure, or didn't see and could do with a little help remembering something. (The genuine need for help empowers our audience rather than simply tests their knowledge.) He's always happy to hear a correct answer and will celebrate success.

HATTY THE HAMSTER – CHARACTER SIDES

Hatty's Arrival:

Good morning, Dave! No, no, no ... that's not right.

(Flips to mock sad.) It's not a good morning. No, it's not.

(Flips to super happy.) It's a great morning! It's a fantastic morning!

You know why...? ... because, today we're going on *(beat of anticipation)* a Circus Adventure! That's why I'm wearing ... a circus hat!

   (He pulls hat out from behind his back and puts it on his head.)

I thought of wearing a circus elephant – but grey isn't my colour.

So, is everyone ready for a Circus Adventure? You are! Great! To your Rollypods!

Here we go! All aboard the Spin-Again for A Circus Adventure!

Sample Question Moments:

Who found the most sheep? Was it Ruff-Ruff, Tweet or Dave? What was that? I can't hear you?

Yes! It was Ruff-Ruff! Ruff-Ruff found three sheep! Tweet found two sheep, and Dave found ... a cow. Dave is a funny blue panda isn't he?

Can you guess who will go to sleep first today? Ruff-Ruff, Tweet or Dave?

It's Dave. It's always Dave.

Until our next adventure. Bye-bye everyone. Bye! See you next time!

Tony and Helen had very clear ideas of what they wanted. Young, bright, lively, but a very personable character, not squeaky and too cartoony. A very real character to interact with the characters on screen and then to turn to camera and interact with the audience.

We tried various different variations in pitch, speed, energy and we came up with a light, very young, but not childlike voice. A pubescent brother sort of voice, but with a slightly more adult personality in that you can trust him. He's kind and generous, but also great fun.

David Holt – The voice of 'Hatty'

Although the scripts have been written and the characters drawn, the complex animation process only begins to take shape once the voice sessions get underway. The animators work closely with the recordings to get their timings and create the numerous drawings that make up the moving images.

However sophisticated the visuals, the human subtleties of facial expression and body language are difficult to replicate in detail. So, for the drawings to come alive, the voices of the characters often have to be heightened. The more you can offer, by way of expression and depth of emotion, the more an animator is inspired.

You may be worried about letting go and making a fool of yourself. Relax, enjoy the experience and don't be afraid. It's rare that you have to rein someone in, you're generally pushing them to go that bit further.

Nick Harris – Engineer/Director

As in other areas of voice work, *listening* is an essential skill.

Many, many months will have been spent planning the production. Every aspect, from the intended audience, the initial storyline, how it will look, how it will sound, where it will be sold, how much it will cost to make and who will play which character will have been discussed at great length and in great detail by the production company and the broadcasters.

The producer and production team will have a very clear idea of what they need to achieve in the recording sessions. So when it's your turn to step up to the mic, *listen* carefully to what it is they're asking for, and work *with* them to produce the performance.

We have to take someone's voice track and animate to that, so if we say it's not big enough ... it's not big enough. Don't just give a subtle performance because you think that's what an actor should give. Listen to the director because they know what they're doing.

Helen Stroud – Animation Producer

Variations of lines, scenes or interactions are often recorded as alternatives and considered later during post-production. If you have ideas, offer them up for discussion. If time is at a premium, however, this may be a luxury that can't be accommodated; animation budgets are frequently stretched. If this is the case, you may have to go with the flow and accept the script as is.

Having a personal collection of voices in your memory will be a useful resource in the creative process. As you go about your life you can build this library by *listening* to the voices around you, both natural and fictional. Note their different styles, accents, ages, backgrounds. Make a note of any unusual mannerisms.

A voiceover we knew went a step further and kept a memo recorder by the television. He logged a whole range of different voices for reference.

As part of the performance you may also need to reproduce a range of vocal effects in the style of the voice you've created. These will be determined by the script, but could include: laughs, cries, coughs, sneezes, burps, moans, snores, eating, drinking etc. In the animation industry these are collectively known as 'walla'.

It's usual for the production team to create a 'walla' library for each character as part of the recording process. They may also record a collective 'walla' effort by the whole cast if specific crowd reactions, such as gasps, ooohs or aaahs are needed.

Each vocal effect opens up another area of development. For example, what type of laugh would your character have; guffaw, contagious, polite, nervous, belly, snorting, cruel, manic? Does it vary depending on the situation they're in?

It's quite possible that you'll be asked to play more than one character in a production, particularly if they are characters that have only have a few scenes or lines.

I've frequently been in a situation where I've played three or four characters and sometimes they all crop up in one scene. Once I get the voices set in my head and I know what they sound like, then I find it relatively easy to hop from one to the other.

David Holt – Voiceover

Recording sessions for an animation film or TV series can often be spread over weeks, months and in some cases years. So once you've established a character's voice, it will need to be sustained and accurately recalled whenever required.

> I remember character voices I create through muscle memory and
> because I'll have really 'got into' each character, I have a visual
> image of them in my mind.

Teresa Gallagher — Voiceover

As the animation film reaches the finishing stages and your character is now moving around on screen, you may be recalled to 'post-sync' specific words or lines that need adding or replacing for one reason or another. With this in mind, it's worth becoming familiar with the skills of dubbing and ADR (see pp. 40-42).

 If you need a reminder of your character's voice, the studio will have a clip from a previous session but you could also keep a sample on your tablet or smartphone.

If a series becomes very popular, items of promotional material or merchandise may be introduced that incorporate the voices of the show's characters. If a suitable line of dialogue can't be found in the original soundtrack, then it's likely you'll be booked again to record a specific script.

Generally speaking the dialogue for a TV series is recorded alongside other members of the cast. This has the benefit of characters being able to react with each other and can sometimes result in a spontaneous and creative performance.

> They have to be together and they have to play off each other so
> they get the pitch and level right and enjoy each other's company.
> There's something you can never get if you record them separately.

Leo Neilsen — Animation Producer

The only unnatural aspect of ensemble recording, specific to animation, is that you have to become adept at not overlapping the dialogue. All conversation overlaps are created after the session during post-production. This allows animators more control over the dialogue and a greater freedom with their timings.

> There are little things to be aware of when working ensemble, like
> knowing when to turn a page, keeping still and keeping quiet when
> it's not your turn to speak. It's all part of the studio craft you need to
> learn.

Nick Harris — Engineer/Director

In the studio you may be standing to perform. This is not unusual for an animation session. Body movement, as long as it doesn't compromise the recording and move you away from the microphone, will help expand the character's voice, as will facial expressions.

> *If you do move around be sure to get your mic technique right. But there's something in the energy that you get by standing up.*

> **Helen Stroud – Animation Producer**

Dialogue for video games is usually recorded individually because there are many permutations of a character's lines that are needed to create the various different outcomes of the story.

If all this sounds appealing then immerse yourself in the many and varied worlds of animation. Children's television is a rich source, with a whole variety of series being broadcast. There are also classic feature films such as those produced by Pixar and Disney. You can also find material online, including behind-the-scenes glimpses of actors performing in front of the microphone.

> *Research is the answer. Watch cartoons, listen to what people are doing, look at the credits to see the people that are there and realise the versatility that's required and what sort of skill level you have to reach to be successful.*

> **Helen Stroud – Animation Producer**

There are many ways to practise and develop skills for animation. Reading children's stories *aloud* is a great place to start. There's a wealth of wonderful characters to vocalise. Study their personalities within the context of the story. Observe how they interact with each other. Notice their size, age, gender and mannerisms.

With a little imagination you can also bring objects around your home to life. How would a salt mill and a pepper mill sound, for example, and how would they interact with each other?

Start with size. Are they tall and slender or short and squat? What effect might that have on how they sound? Where would their voices be pitched? Would their speaking tempos be different? Does the fact that one contains spicy pepper and the other tangy salt have an impact on where their voices come from physically (nasal, top of the skull, back of the mouth etc.)? What is their back story? If you gave some thought earlier about how your own voice evolved and all the influences that affected it, consider now what imaginary events may have shaped these characters.

Character development is essential. It's the difference between just reading words off the page, and turning them into actual speech and emotion — what the character is thinking, and doing, and about to do, and has just done.

David Holt — Voiceover

As you focus on this area of work, begin to create a cast of character styles on which you can draw when working on a new project. Have in mind, or better still write down, their vocal attributes. Try them out by recording and playing back. This will certainly heighten your awareness of what your voice can and can't do. Over time you can develop these characters by changing their age, accent or mood.

MP3 Auditions

As you saw from the Collingwood & Co experience, once a brief is sent out to agents, such is the interest and eagerness to get involved with a production that hundreds of MP3 auditions could be received.

Many smartphones have the facility to create and email audio files, but if yours doesn't have this feature then it's worth investing in a reasonable quality USB microphone for your laptop or tablet. Either way, it would clearly be an asset to teach yourself to record, save and email auditions.

Whilst they may be fairly basic recordings in terms of quality, these audio auditions are nonetheless an opportunity to impress the producers and get your foot in the door. So consider the brief carefully and make your offering the best it can be!

Dubbing

Compared with France, Italy, Germany and Spain dubbing is not a major industry in Britain. There are no 'stars' of the dubbing world as there are in these countries. The majority of our imported film and TV series come from America and those that do originate in Europe are often subtitled, as in terms of production this is a cheaper option. There are exceptions, however, notably animation.

The process of dubbing is used to replace the original dialogue of a character in a film or video with another language or accent. It will invariably include grunts, moans, laughter and other human noises and reactions.

It's sometimes known as 're-versioning' and will always be recorded 'to picture'. It's also known as 'lip-sync' simply because it involves matching lip movement with spoken word.

When you're dubbing, your performance is restricted by the performance that somebody else has already given. So you've no latitude for ad-libbing and the timing is set in stone with very little or no variation. It's a totally artificial position to be in when you're trying to create and perform as a character.

David Holt – Voiceover

The process is quite complex and, as a performer, there's a lot to contend with. While maintaining the voice you've been booked to replace and following a script, there may be a soundtrack or foreign voice in your headphones and visual cues that signal when to begin and end the dialogue.

The performance on screen has to be followed exactly to remain faithful to the original sound. The aim is to have the viewer believe that the character they're watching, actually spoke in that particular accent or language.

It takes a lot of skill and co-ordination; as a dubbing voiceover you have to be adept at multi-tasking.

If I see people with potential I may start them off with a re-versioning series going from American English into UK English or Australian into UK English where the lip-sync is much easier to hit. So they see how the whole thing works.

Tony Church – Producer

Studios use a variety of methods to cue a voiceover in exactly the right place. There may be time-code in vision (see p. 52), a series of beeps (1, 2, 3 and speak on the 4th), streamers (a vertical or slanted line that travels from left to right across the screen – when it hits the right edge of the screen, you are on cue), or a visual countdown.

Another method used extensively in France is called 'La Bande Rythmo'. This technology shows the words that are being replaced along the bottom of the screen. The text is synchronised with the picture and stretches or contracts to reflect the mouth movements of the on-screen actor or character. This method makes for a more productive session and has been updated in more recent dubbing software. There are many examples to be found online.

If you are going to do dubbing try and work with mouth movements and mimic what's being said.

Tony Church – Producer

ADR

Automated Dialogue Replacement, also known as '**looping**' or '**post-sync**', is different from dubbing in that it's always recorded in the originating language. It's a process that happens during post-production if the original lines recorded on the set or location are compromised, or if the director decides, for some reason, that the original voice needs to be replaced. The techniques involved are quite similar to dubbing.

The term 'looping' refers to the short section being played over and over again in a loop, with the original sound played through headphones. This helps you get into the rhythm of the words and the spirit of the original performance. It will help if you can memorise the dialogue of the scene being replaced so you can ignore the script and concentrate on the screen to see how the voice fits the character.

The challenge is to make the words believable within the context of the scene. You need to respond to the situation and if, for example, the character is making a movement, then you also need to physically react.

Audiobooks

Reading audiobooks is a unique area of voice work.

A passion for reading and enjoyment of the process is essential, as it requires a great deal of concentration and preparation. It can be a very rewarding experience, particularly if you have a talent for accents and creating characters.

> *Make sure your accents are authentic and up to scratch, and never offer to do an accent you are not 100% sure of — you will be caught out at some point.*
>
> **Tamsin Collinson — Audiobook Director**

There are two distinct reading styles; the first, where all the characters are vocally differentiated, and the second, where the text is read as narrative.

Recording sessions require a good deal of groundwork, the more so if you've not had a lot of experience. Whatever time is set aside for the recording, it's reasonable to suggest you'll need roughly two and a half times that for your preparation. So, a three-day recording session would take about eight days to prepare.

You may have to read the whole book two, three or four times. The first to get an overview of the story, plot and characters, the second to create a cast list and establish voices for each character, possibly a third for rehearsal and the fourth for the recording itself.

It's essential to read out loud during all of your preparation. Accents, dialogue or narrative simply don't work in your head.

> *I prepare the whole of my book out loud, because that's what I'm going to be doing. And if you don't, it's going to take you by surprise when you get into the studio.*
>
> **Christian Rodska – Voiceover**

During your second read-through, begin marking it up in a way that works for you. Some voiceovers, for example, use different colour highlighters to identify individual characters.

> *It helps to initial lines of dialogue in a scene where several characters are speaking, so that you are sure of who says what.*
>
> **Tamsin Collinson – Audiobook Director**

If there's a producer working on the project they may have an artistic input and offer consultation, otherwise it'll generally be your choice as to how the characters are portrayed. You may find it useful to form mental pictures of what they look like and the scenes in which they find themselves. Just as in animation, make sure you can sustain a character's voice without harming your voice.

During your preparation be sure to check all pronunciations and, if needs be, write down phonetic approximations on the script.

 There are many websites that offer audio pronunciation of words. Make sure they are UK English.

Studio sessions require stamina – vocal and physical. They are generally seven or eight hours long and, depending on the length of book, may run over several days. Pace yourself where you can. If you have sections that are complicated or emotive then consider the best time of the day to record them. The aim is to sound as fresh at the end of the day as you did at the beginning.

> *They are long days. It's very demanding and not an easy ride. Often it's the mental concentration that catches you out more than the vocal stamina.*
>
> **David Holt – Voiceover**

Good sight-reading skills will again prove invaluable. The text has to be read accurately with only the slightest variation in direct speech, for example 'He's' instead of 'He is.'

Just as in any other area of voice work, if you enjoy the performance and become engaged with what you're reading, you will draw the listener in.

You're telling a story; enjoy it, communicate it to the listener.

Christian Rodska – Voiceover

There's lots of free output available, particularly on BBC Radio. Spend time *listening* and becoming familiar with a variety of content.

Other Work

So far we have talked about what's generally considered core work for a voiceover, but there are other areas where voice skills are also employed.

Sponsorship Idents

On commercial TV channels these are the short announcements letting you know that the programme you're watching, or are about to watch, is sponsored by a particular company or product.

Corporate Projects

The internet has provided the opportunity for companies to train or inform staff while at their desks rather than attending seminars. Similarly, business customers can be informed of services or marketing opportunities on a company's website.

This work can, however, prove quite challenging, as the scripts will have a noticeably different style from programme narration. They are likely to be written from a more formal business perspective and may include language, terminology and jargon pertinent to that particular industry.

It's finding the right voice to talk to the people that you want,
in a way in which you want to make a relationship with them,
irrespective of the platform. Catching your ear is what it's all about.

Pam Myers – Producer

Voice Commands

These are heard in a wide variety of applications to guide or inform: satnav, aircraft cockpit, smart cars, lifts, public transport, self-service etc.

Auto-Attendant

The Auto-Attendant has been widely adopted by many companies to allow callers to be directed to the right department without the need for a dedicated phone operator. Professional voiceovers are often used in preference to employees because of their skills in making quite ordinary information sound interesting.

Animatics

Making a TV commercial is expensive, so an advertising agency will go to great lengths to ensure they're on the right track. They use short videos, known as an 'animatics', to test their concept with various focus groups and get vital feedback. They feature a series of key scenes from the commercial, drawn as storyboards or created using computer animation. A soundtrack is added and this often includes a voiceover describing the action. Such as ...

'We see a man getting out of a car, he turns to walk away.
As he does so, he turns to lock the doors with his key fob.'

There are many examples to be found online. Just type in 'animatics'. Given the economical nature of this type of project, you may get to voice more than one character. And, because animatics are not broadcast, it's often an opportunity for a producer to try a voiceover they've not used before.

English Language Training Courses

These are generally a collection of short audio scenarios to assist the learning of English as a spoken language. They also provide the opportunity to play several different characters.

Continuity Announcing

A continuity announcer is the voice heard between TV and radio programmes. Their job is to hook the viewer, entice them to stay with the channel on to the next programme or tune in again later in the day. At the end of a programme, they may give out information such as any merchandise relating to the show or provide details of organisations who may offer support in relation to a storyline or issue raised in the programme.

Continuity announcements are either pre-recorded or live and presenters often write their own scripts. An acute sense of timing is essential.

It's a wonderful job and that very rare thing in the business; a regular gig!

Deidre Mullins – Voiceover and Continuity Presenter

... coming up next, Part Three.

PART THREE
THE STUDIO

PART THREE – THE STUDIO

This is where it all comes together.

Before we describe what happens in a typical recording session, we will explain some of the technical aspects that affect your performance and also the personal preparation you need to consider.

A recording studio generally consists of two adjoining rooms. The clients and sound engineer operate from the control room; this is separated by a window from the voice booth where you'll be performing. The size of this room varies considerably; from palatial, to something the size of a broom cupboard. It'll also be soundproofed, which gives it a very 'dead' feel and often there's not a lot of natural light.

For the majority of sessions you'll be seated. But there are exceptions, most notably in animation work where standing is often preferred.

Technicalities

It's the sound engineer's job to deal with all the sophisticated audio equipment and get the best possible recording of your voice, but it can make a big difference if you know a few basic techniques that will enhance your performance.

A professional microphone (or 'mic' for short) is highly sensitive and directional; only picking up sound from an area to the front.

It's important to be aware of this, because if you get so absorbed with your performance that you drift away from this area your voice will begin to sound woolly and indistinct and the engineer will let you know you're 'off mic'. As you will be working quite close to the microphone any small movement is greatly magnified, so it's important to be consistent. As you become more experienced you will hear in the headphones if this happens.

So, how should you approach a microphone? How far away from the front should you be?

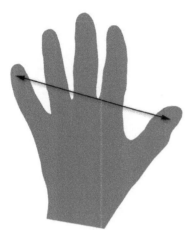

For most general reads 18 cm or 7 inches is about right. This is approximately the span of an open hand. If you have a particularly soft or loud voice then you can move in or away accordingly. The engineer will always guide you.

Generally though if the script requires a warm, intimate read then you'd move closer; the nearer you get to a microphone, the warmer your voice sounds (known as the 'proximity effect'.)

If the words demand a loud delivery then pulling back a little will help, but take care not to overdo it or again you'll sound 'off mic'.

 Microphone technique is an acquired skill and will become second nature over time.

 Microphones are very sensitive; never be tempted to tap or blow into them for any reason.

Pops

Some consonants, most notably **P**, **T** and **K** sounds, have a nasty habit of 'exploding' onto the microphone and creating a plosive or 'pop' sound.

To give you some idea of the energy created, put the palm of your hand about 10cm in front of your mouth and say the word 'pop'. Even said quite gently you can feel the air pressure hitting your palm. Replace your hand with a sensitive microphone and that pressure is translated into an explosive 'pop'. It becomes particularly exaggerated if you're aiming for a warm, intimate read and speaking very close to the mic.

A 'pop shield' is frequently used to dissipate consonant energy, but you can also learn to minimise 'poping'. Try turning your head *slightly* away from the mic and speak across it when a problem consonant appears. This diverts the air stream away from the sensitive diaphragm.

Alternatively, hold a finger in front of, but not touching, your mouth as if you were shushing someone. Using this last technique, try the pop test on your hand again and feel the reduced blast of air!

Away from the microphone you can practise by using the 'hand in front of mouth' technique. Repeat the consonants **P**, **T** and **K** until you are forming them accurately without the air pressure blasting on to the palm of your hand.

Move on to whole words containing these consonants and then phrases so that you learn to make these sounds within the context of fluent speech. Use tongue twisters such as

'Peter Piper picked a peck of pickled peppers' etc.

Sibilance

Sibilance has many causes, but primarily it's to do with the position of the front of the tongue, jaw setting and the air flow. Sibilance is often heard as a whistley 'S' or such as the consonant sound which occurs in the middle of the word 'solicitor'. Sibilant consonants have a characteristically intense sound on the microphone. It can be hard to eliminate as a speech characteristic, but if you're particularly worried by this issue then seek out the specialist help of a voice coach or speech language therapist.

As with 'pops' you can soften the effect by speaking across the microphone. If the sibilance is very persistent the engineer may reduce it technically with a 'de-esser', but this can often flatten the sound.

It should be said that sibilance and 'pops' are both common characteristics of speech and are not something you should worry about excessively.

Headphones

Headphones (also known as 'cans') are essential in a session. They allow you to hear your own voice and any other sounds related to your performance. These may be other artists in the booth with you, a music track, sound effects, a guide voice-track or the talkback from the control room.

It's always best to wear cans unless it inhibits the performance. A good voiceover will always be listening to themselves, so they know if they've popped or gone off mic.

Dave Peacock — Producer/Engineer

Most studios provide closed-back, over-the-ear headphones. If you're not used to wearing this type, then it can be an unusual sensation, you suddenly feel cut off from the world and your voice can sound a little artificial. If this is your experience then try wearing one earpiece on and one off. This will allow you to get a balance between how the microphone hears your voice and how you're used to hearing it.

It's really a personal preference; try both ways and get a feel for which works for you.

I like to wear 'cans' — headphones; it helps to know how you sound and it makes you aware of the small noises in the throat, tummy, script rustle, which have to be eradicated. The microphone is seldom selective, it hears everything and is unforgiving if extraneous noises are made.

Miriam Margolyes - Voiceover

If however, you adopt the 'one on, one off' method, then be sure the earpiece that's not over your ear is clamped securely to your head. This is to avoid any sound coming through the headphones being picked up by the microphone. The engineer will let you know if this happens, so you can make an adjustment.

 It's important that you're comfortable with the overall volume and the balance between your voice and any other sounds. Most studios have an optimum set-up; that said, if anything needs a slight adjustment then don't hesitate to ask the engineer.

Recording Wild / To Picture

There are two modes of recording your voice: 'Wild' or 'To Picture.

When you're recording 'wild' there's no picture or soundtrack to react to.

When recording 'to picture' the images you need to speak along to will be seen on a TV monitor in the booth. This system is most often used when recording TV commercials, TV trailers and documentary narration. Here you have to develop an ability to read and occasionally look up at the screen without losing your place.

There may be occasions when you begin the session working 'to picture' and once you've established a rhythm, switch to recording 'wild'. This is more likely when recording a short-form script.

 If you're working 'to picture' ask to see the film or a section of it in the control room so that you can begin to absorb the 'clues' to the 'read' from the images. Graphics, music, sound effects are much more potent on the larger screen and speakers.

Working 'wild' is easier, but working with picture is good, because it gives you a sense of the nearly finished film so you can adjust your delivery according to the pace and feel of the piece you're doing.

David Holt – Voiceover

Going for a 'Take'

A 'take' is the name given to a piece of text or action that has been recorded. Each time the same piece is recorded it is given a different take number; take one, take two etc.

You'll always be given a cue to begin speaking. If you're recording 'wild' this may simply be the engineer announcing the take number, or there may be a cue light ...

Whichever method is used, leave a beat and start speaking.

How will you know when to start speaking if you're working to picture?

If there's any sync-sound, it's usually shown on the script. You will hear the soundtrack in the headphones and often take your cues from the end of sync-sound to the beginning of the next. Or you may be given a cue light to begin the next section of text.

Alternatively, a series of numbers, known as 'time-code' may be displayed at the top or bottom of the picture showing hours, minutes, seconds and frames (you can happily ignore the frames; at 25 per second these are simply too fast to register). It gives a point of reference throughout the programme. Scripts may have the time-code entry points at the start of each section of narration which gives you a clue as to whether the words are fitting the pictures. Although less used with modern technology, you may still come across it, particularly in animation sessions, so it's worth a mention.

HOURS : MINS : SECS : FRAMES

A3 Sometimes a rough recording of the script is made specifically for timing purposes. Known as a 'guide track', this is played through the headphones for you to take your cues from. It takes a little getting used to, but once you get into the rhythm it's fairly straightforward.

The method of cueing will always be established at the start of the session. In time you'll intuitively recognise the signs to begin.

Before the Session

Bookings

Agents will all have their own idiosyncratic ways of running their businesses. So this is a rough guide as to how you actually arrive at a booking.

Someone calling your agent to make a booking is referred to as the **Client**. The call may come from an advertising agency, a production company, TV channel, radio station or from the corporate sector and others.

The client will have selected your voice either by listening to voice clips on the website or by ringing your agent with a brief and asking for suggestions.

Once they have made their choice and booked a studio, they will call to make a provisional booking – this is known as a 'pencil'. You will often hear voiceovers say 'I'm on a pencil'.

Your agent will let you know about the 'pencil'. If you accept the provisional booking then you have in effect agreed to keep that time free. At some stage it will either be confirmed or cancelled.

Be aware that in the frantic world of advertising a 'pencil' is often not confirmed until the last minute! But until you hear one way or another it's best to assume the time is booked.

Availability

Your agent will always need to know your availability. If, therefore, you're going on holiday, have a doctor's appointment or any other commitment, let them know as soon as possible. Even if you *think* you might not be available on a certain day, flag it up.

How Long Does a Session Last?

You will generally be booked for a minimum of one hour. The length of a session is very much determined by what type of script is being recorded. A thirty-second commercial may take less than an hour, whereas a two-hour documentary could take three or longer.

Whatever the length of the booking, consider yourself at the client's disposal for the entire duration, even if you've previously experienced similar sessions finishing early.

> *You're there for the hour to deliver what they ask for. Even if they've got what they want, they may want to try something different. You're offering them a service at the end of the day.*
>
> *Sue Elliott-Nicholls – Voiceover*

Overruns

It's sometimes difficult to estimate how much time is needed to record a particular script. So you may find yourself booked for an hour with half an hour's 'overrun'. This simply means the client has an option to keep you for the extra time if needs be. This is a way of managing the budget and giving the producer flexibility.

There will be occasions when the allotted time runs out; perhaps there are technical hitches or problems with the script. If the studio is able to accommodate the extra time needed and you've no immediate commitments, then you can stay and finish the job, particularly if you're in full flow. If this happens, then be sure to let your agent know so the client's invoice can be amended accordingly.

Fees and Usage

Voiceover work is generally based on a standard hourly fee, and there are set rates for the different types of work, which your agent will explain to you in greater detail.

For commercial work there is often a usage fee attached. For TV, this is based on where the commercial is shown and how often. For radio it's based on which stations it is played on.

Bear in mind there are *no guarantees* of your recording being used. You should never rely on earning any more than your session fee – perhaps consider the usage fee as a bonus!

Session Etiquette

Approaching your work in a professional manner is essential.

It's important that you spend time warming up your voice before a session; *especially* if it's an early-morning start. When you sit in front of a microphone you must be ready to perform.

Many of us have to clear mucus from our throats. If you're particularly prone to this you may have to avoid certain foods such as dairy products. Coffee may also produce 'frogginess' or a dry mouth. This can result in 'mouth noise' as you speak and can be impossible for the engineer to eliminate.

Give some thought as to the clothes you wear. This is a practical consideration as the rustle of some fabrics can be picked up by the sensitive microphone.

 There's a short vocal warm-up routine on pp. 84-89.

Take water with you and have something to eat before, because tummy rumbles are not good in the middle of a session.

Bethan James – Voiceover

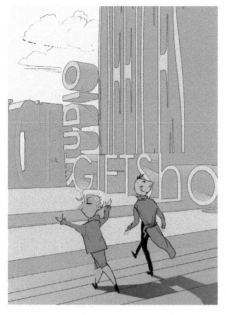

It must be here somewhere?

Make sure you're familiar with the location of the studio you're working in that day. This may sound obvious, until you realise the entrance could be an anonymous front door in a road that may be a mile long. Others may even be some distance out of town.

Arriving late, tense and without sufficient time to settle your voice is counterproductive even for the most seasoned voiceover. Crucially, you may end up costing the client extra money in studio fees if, as a result of you being late, they have to book extra time to finish the job.

If there was one piece of advice we heard over and over again from agents, producers and engineers it was, 'Don't be late'.

Aim to arrive five to ten minutes before the start of a session. Take a moment to centre yourself. As we've said, for most commercial or TV trailer work you won't have the script in advance. If you arrive in good time there's a chance you'll get to see it before going into the studio. This is a precious opportunity not to be wasted.

 If you're feeling tense this will have an adverse effect on your voice. Use a basic relaxation method. Release your abdominal muscles and allow your breath to drop down deep into your body.

The Session

Every session will be a slightly different experience. It will vary, depending on the material you're recording and the people attending the session.

Working with the Client

If a sound studio is a new experience, then be assured there's nothing to worry about, staff always aim to create a comfortable, relaxed environment.

When you arrive at reception be sure you know the details of your job:

> The production company or advertising agency
>
> The producer
>
> The product

Also ask the name of the engineer you'll be working with.

> *It's very important for me to have a relationship with the engineer.*
> *They're the mediator between the client and what you're doing*
> *and they can be very helpful in dispelling any kind of fears you've*
> *got about whether you're doing something wrong or not.*
>
> **Teresa Gallagher – Voiceover**

If you haven't previously worked for the client, be confident in knowing that you're there because, having heard your showreel, they like the sound of your voice.

> *If you're nervous, say so and we'll help you through. Nervousness*
> *can come across as arrogance and you might leave everyone with*
> *the wrong impression.*
>
> **Tim Lofts – Engineer**

The number of people attending a session varies enormously depending on what you're recording. But typically, in a commercial session, there'll be the Producer, a Production Assistant (PA), the agency creative team (Copywriter and Art Director) and often a representative from the company whose product is being advertised.

> *When you walk into the studio remember that everyone in the*
> *room is working towards the same thing at the end of the day.*
>
> **Nick Harris – Engineer/ Director**

A key ingredient of a successful session will be your relationship with the assembled team and especially the producer and sound engineer. It's a good idea to create a rapport with everyone. Try to remember their names or write them on the side of your script.

If you get on well with everyone and produce a performance they're happy with, then you will very likely meet them again. Most clients have their favourite artists and cast them, not just because they get the job done quickly and efficiently, but because they also contribute to the session and are enthusiastic and pleasant to work with. Personality plays a big part in the success of a voiceover.

Being 'studio savvy' certainly oils the tracks for future work. What you say 'off mic' is probably as important as the scripted stuff.

Bob Golding – Voiceover

It's unlikely you will go straight into the booth. There's usually a moment or two spent breaking the ice which helps create a good working atmosphere. Once the introductions are over the producer will brief you about the script and explain what they want from you.

In order for you to convey what's needed, you first have to *listen* to what's needed.

You've got to work out the unsaid of what they actually want from a script. I think that intuition is something you develop after more and more jobs.

Nico Lennon – Voiceover

Apart from the scenario, target audience and style, you may also be given clues such as …'we liked your voice because …', or 'we heard such and such on your showreel.' If they mention a particular track that led them to choose you, keep referring to it in your mind as a point of reference.

This is also your first opportunity to ASK any questions you may have about the script or the character you're playing. Asking questions is essential.

All this will help you to perform at your best from the start.

Listen to your showreel from time to time just to refresh your memory.

While you should always refer to the producer for guidance, be aware that other members of the 'team' may also be offering an opinion throughout the session. Part of your skill will be to judge what's needed from a variety of voices.

That said, don't hesitate to ask if, at any time, you're not sure about a particular instruction. Asking for clarification may also help them to focus on what it is they're looking for.

There can be lots of discussion between the creative team in the control room as the session progresses. You may have to wait until these resolve into a specific direction.

The worse thing a voiceover can do is try and react to every bit of information they hear. Best to sit back and wait. Refer to the producer or even the engineer who will often sift information for you.

Pam Myers — Producer

From time to time you may come across, what you consider to be, a poorly written script. It's worth remembering that before landing in your hands it will have been through a very rigorous journey of approval. The client may also have certain preferences about pronunciations that conflict with yours.

Whatever your thoughts, it's best not to appear negative. Clients may not take too kindly to any adverse comments, directly or indirectly, so try to be constructive.

If you're finding it difficult to read or it's not particularly well written, what you mustn't do is sound annoyed by it or look down on it.

Christopher Kent — Producer

In the Voice Booth

Be sure to turn your mobile off; not just to silent or airplane mode. Signals can interfere with recordings as can the vibrate mode or any reminders you've set. Remove any jangly jewellery or watches with loud ticks; extraneous noises can easily be picked up by the sensitive microphone.

You'll generally find a table, chair, headphones, microphone, TV monitor, cue light and possibly some kind of lectern on which to rest your script. More often than not there will also be notepads, pencils and tissues, but it's always worth carrying your own with you just in case. A small bottle of water will also be valuable.

 Gulping down water may make your stomach rumble so only take small sips.

Establish as best you can a line of communication. If you can see the person directing you through the window, so much the better.

Remember, that in the control room everyone can always hear you, but you'll only hear them when they have something to say, so there may be periods of silence from time to time as they discuss things.

Don't be afraid of the silence. When they turn off the talkback it can be a very lonely place if you're sitting there for three or four minutes while they're obviously talking about things. Often though what they're talking about is nothing directly to do with you.

Ben Fairman — Producer

There are exceptions; some studios operate what's known as an 'open-mic' policy. In this instance you will hear everything that's being said in the control room.

Once you've had time to settle in, the engineer will adjust the microphone so it's in the ideal position. Be sure you're seated comfortably so their adjustments suit you, rather than the other way around. Once satisfied and back in the control room, s/he will ask you to read the script for 'level' (that's the volume of your voice). It's important that you do this in the manner that you intend to read the actual take, indeed count this as a valuable rehearsal.

Voice work need not be a static affair; some small movements, without straying away from the microphone or compromising the recording in any way, may help give an expressive read.

> *It's very easy to drift off-mic when recording, so always check your position and if necessary, ask your engineer to check that you are fully 'present' on mic.*

Miriam Margolyes – Voiceover

Once the session starts you might record several takes before anyone makes a comment. This is usual. Everyone is listening to your interpretation of the script to see how it matches theirs. It gives the producer a valuable reference point from which to work and provides you an opportunity to warm into the script.

 It's often better to give a bigger performance than you think is necessary. It's unlikely to be as 'over the top' as you imagine and, it's generally agreed that, it's easier to pull back a performance than it is to raise one.

As the session progresses you'll hear various 'takes' played back. *Listen* carefully to your performance and any notes or adjustments that are given. Once again, don't be afraid to ask if you're not clear what you're being directed to do.

> *Don't panic — it's easy to feel out of your depth. If you're not sure ask — there's nothing worse than not understanding and thinking 'maybe I'll just try and wing it', because it doesn't work.*

Bethan James — Voiceover

At the same time as making these small changes, you have to keep the underlying performance consistent. This is important, as the final edit may comprise of various 'takes'. This consistency includes maintaining your position on the microphone.

> Consistency doesn't mean simply doing the same thing over and over again. It means that once you're in a particular range, stay there. Try a few things out but stay there. If I've got two very contrasting takes I can't put anything together.
>
> **Pam Myers – Producer**

During playback you may notice things about your performance that you feel could be improved. Don't feel inhibited, make suggestions; it's all part of the creative collaboration.

> If they don't like the way you've done something it doesn't mean you've got it wrong. It just means it's not what they imagined. Don't get bogged down with thinking they don't like you, don't get paranoid. Also, there may be several people in the room who want to try different ideas.
>
> **Sue Elliott-Nicholls – Voiceover**

Once the client feels they have a 'take' they're happy with, go into the control room and suggest you *listen* to it on the big speakers. This is a final opportunity to check your performance.

Something a high-profile voiceover once said to us however, is that 'You'll always think of a better way to say it ... on the way home'.

Fluffs and Pick-ups

You won't always give a perfect 'read' and from time to time you'll make mistakes or 'fluffs', as they are affectionately known. As long as everyone is happy with the overall recording, the sound engineer can edit sections of different 'takes' together to make a satisfying whole.

Occasionally, you may be asked to record a '**pick-up**'. This is usually a line or short section that everyone feels could be improved. It will be recorded wild and edited into the master take. Sometimes you will be asked to read it two or three times 'on the trot'. This is an opportunity to get into the flow and give the clients a choice.

Sometimes the engineer will deal with any edits as the recording progresses, particularly if it's a long-form script. So, if you 'fluff' a word or rustle the script, s/he will go back to a convenient point in the recording before the error. You will then hear what you previously recorded in the headphones and at an agreed point, usually the end of a phrase, s/he will drop into record mode and you will continue reading once again. It's a quick and efficient way to achieve a seamless voice track at the end of the session.

 It's important, however, to 'pick-up' without snatching at your breath and also with the same energy and pace of your read to that point. A good way to achieve this is to read along with yourself as the engineer plays you into the pick-up.

Copies or 'Lifts'

If at the end of a session you feel it was a particularly good performance or in a style not represented on your showreel, then consider asking the producer for a copy or 'lift'. It's very rare to be denied unless it's either a test or a pitch, but you may have to wait until after the recording has been broadcast.

You might consider getting some simple business cards printed with a photograph and email address, which you can give to the engineer so s/he can send you an MP3 file.

PART FOUR

THE BUSINESS

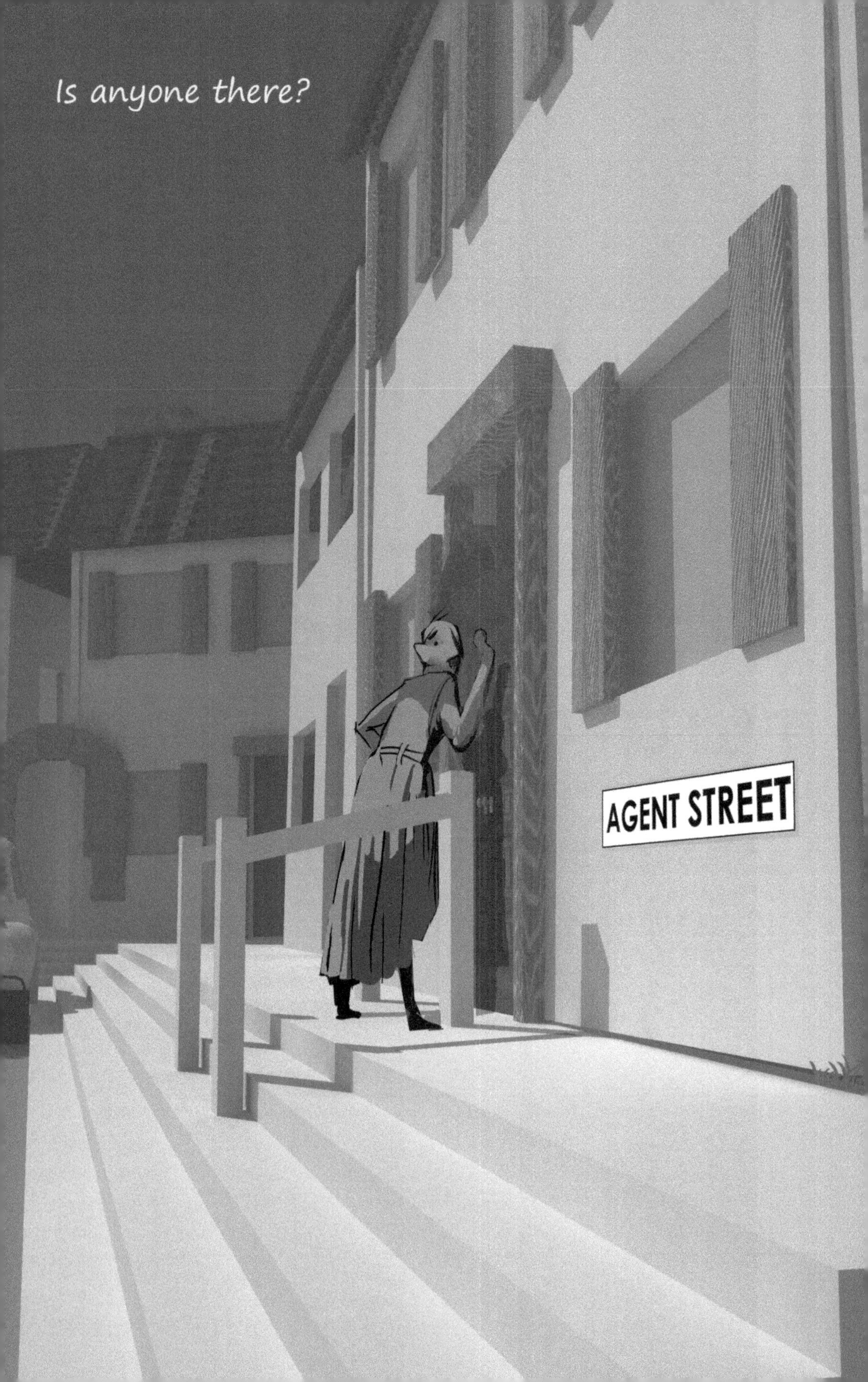
Is anyone there?
AGENT STREET

PART FOUR – THE BUSINESS

What you need to get started – the business of voiceovers.

Knowing your Strengths

It's now important to consider what your strong points are and what type of work might suit you. Every voiceover has their particular strengths – it's rare for any artist to be skilled in every aspect of the business. Some are good at character voices, but not straight reads. Some prefer short-form rather than long. Others are better suited to narrative, but not technical jargon and so on.

> *Not everybody can do character voices and we discourage it unless they are very, very good.*
>
> **Sue Terry – Voice Agent**

You may inevitably start out by recording commercials, because it's the most obvious way into the world of voiceovers. Over time, however, it's possible you will find your strengths lie in other areas.

What's more, working as a voiceover will undoubtedly bring challenges that will stretch your vocal boundaries and revise your thinking about your voice and what it will do.

> *The market chooses you. You may think that you're great at commercials or you're great at animation, but the market might decide you're a great documentary voice.*
>
> **Maxine Wiltshire – Voice Agent**

ONE Voice

It's a commonly held belief that to be a voiceover you have to be endlessly versatile and produce a broad range of accents and character voices.

An array of skills will inevitably extend your job opportunities, but having just one voice is not a barrier, far from it. The majority of voice work demands a natural and authentic voice that is flexible enough to include a variety of different read styles; energised, soft, informative, funny, sympathetic etc. Think of a paint chart. You might decide you have a 'blue' voice. Then you realise that there are many shades of that colour.

Knowing how to adapt your voice quickly and effectively is key.

> *I need emotional versatility.*
>
> **Martin Sims – Producer**

Character Voices

If you have an ear for accents and can modify your voice substantially, then of course it will open up a world of opportunities in animation films, audiobooks, video games etc. But as we said earlier, the skills needed are very specific.

Most of us can do the odd line in a funny voice, but ask yourself if you can *sustain* a particular voice, impersonation or accent. Also can you do that voice with a range of emotions?

 Spend some time watching and *listening* to a wide variety of material from the genre.

> *I think you might do well if you have a good vocal range, it certainly gives you the option to play around with every kind of read, but animation work tends to call upon the more extreme recesses of that range.*
>
> **Bob Golding – Voiceover**

Are you sure?

It may be, that even after having read this book, you're still not 100% certain if this work is for you. Launching straight into making a showreel, which many people do, is an expensive way of finding out!

Instead, look for a company that offers the chance to 'give it a try'. This might be as a workshop or an individual audition and should be a relatively cost-effective way of exploring how it feels to work in a studio. You may also get some valuable feedback about your voice and its potential.

> Before you even consider approaching an agent, certainly before you consider getting a showreel done professionally, get yourself in front of a microphone. Get yourself used to hearing the sound of your own voice. Write down ads from the TV and see if you can read it in the same amount of time. Practise, practise, practise.
>
> **Jane Savage – Voice Agent**

Showreels

All voiceovers have a showreel (or voicereel, as it's sometimes known) and it usually features a montage of commercial clips, as advertising is traditionally the most popular and lucrative area of work. As you become more experienced however, you may need to create other showreels that demonstrate skills such as narration, animation, audiobooks etc.

The initial purpose of a showreel is to attract an agent. Once you've been offered representation, the agency will then use it to promote you to their clients.

While it can be expensive to have a showreel made, it's fundamental to the job and therefore should be considered an investment in the business of being a voiceover.

Agents and clients alike will assess you by it. So, from the outset, it's important to spend time and energy getting the best result possible in order to make the best impression. Quality should *never* be compromised; you must be entirely satisfied with the content, your performance and the overall sound.

There are pitfalls to be avoided, so we'll guide you through the process and offer suggestions.

> The overriding thing is the quality of the reel. Usually I can tell in 10 or 15 seconds whether the artist is any good or not.
>
> **Johnny Garcia – Voice Agent**

Where to Record a Showreel

In his time at an artist's agency David heard hundreds of reels from people seeking representation; the reels were often mediocre.

While some people clearly needed better direction or more practice, others should have been given some honest advice about the potential of their voice and the chances of success. Other reels suffered from poor-quality recordings, or a lack of the most basic production values.

Before you begin, spend time researching. *Listen* to the showreels on agency websites, get a broad feel for what's needed and the standard of production that's generally expected.

It's important when having a showreel made that you choose someone with experience to put it together for you. There are a growing number of 'specialist' companies that advertise online. Alternatively, you could approach a post-production studio. Their experienced sound engineers often make showreels in their own time and generally have a feel for what's required.

Take your time and consider carefully who to work with. *Listen* to examples of recent work and, if you have the opportunity, speak to one of their clients; a personal recommendation is always valuable.

Here's a list of considerations when choosing who makes your reel:

- Meet with them to see if you have a rapport.
- Establish what's included in the price and what you'll take away with you.
- Will they provide scripts or will you?
- Make certain you'll be given direction in the studio. It's very hard to direct yourself when you're experienced, let alone when you're just starting out.
- Establish how much studio time you'll have. It's surprisingly tiring work, particularly before it all becomes second nature. There's a lot to think about and a great deal of energy required to give a good performance. You shouldn't feel rushed or under pressure.
- Avoid being overambitious with how much material you record. Even if there are cost implications, it's better to record a few scripts well and come back for another session to finish, if that's an option.

What to Record?

There's no hard and fast rule about how many scripts to record, but aim to demonstrate a contrast of pace, energy and mood; five or six is generally about right. Such is the requirement for authenticity there's little value including a wide range of accents. That said, a demonstration of something neutral will always be useful. This is where knowing yourself will pay off.

Although studios and production companies may supply scripts, it's still worth doing your own research. The more you know about your voice, its strengths and limitations, the better result you'll achieve. It's important to identify the right material to record.

 A common mistake is to think that your voice is suited to every script and every type of product.

If you're working with a director they'll have some input, but the self-knowledge process we described earlier will really pay off now and give you confidence to help choose the right scripts.

> *You can't do everything, you can do some things well and that's what you should do.*
>
> **Kate Davie – Voice Agent**

Throughout this process remain true to what you discovered your voice will do. For example, if you don't particularly relate to humorous material then avoid comic scripts.

The more you *listen* to commercial breaks the easier it'll be to identify which of the commercial sectors suit you. You'll also begin to notice a number of conventions. For example; a lightweight voice is unlikely to promote the latest action movie, likewise a dark, husky voice will probably not be booked to read a baby-care commercial.

 There's a list of commercial sectors under Terminology.

Trends and conventions tend to change over time, so it's worth keeping up to date with what's going on.

> *Quite often you hear voices pushed into using a script that is just not suitable and would never work in the real market.*
>
> **Maxine Wiltshire – Voice Agent**

Once you've broadly identified the type of commercials you feel suit you and you have a variety of styles, copy out the words. It's quite a skill writing a good piece of copy and we feel it's better to use actual broadcast material to give your showreel an air of authenticity.

 Check to see if there are subtitles.

> *... or you have the problem of artists writing their own scripts.*
> *Usually fatal, copywriting is a very specific skill.*
>
> **Johnny Garcia – Voice Agent**

It's best to avoid products that are heavily associated with a celebrity voice; it will be very difficult for the listener to distance themselves from that association.

Find ten or so scripts that offer the moods and styles suited to your vocal range so you have a choice once you get into the studio. Then, with the help of your engineer/director, you can work through them to find which you perform best.

If you include an obvious 'sales' read, also demonstrate a more 'real' person read; a mum, dad, brother, sister, boyfriend, girlfriend, for example. If you have a regional accent then you *may* also want to demonstrate a more neutral accent.

If you decide to record a script that includes dialogue between two people, be sure the other character is of the opposite gender. Two voices of the same sex on a showreel can confuse the listener.

Particularly avoid scripts where your voice needs to be treated, for example, down a phone or through a PA system at a train station. Hearing a 'filtered' voice is a waste of precious space on your reel and rarely of any value.

Showreels should always be of a high standard with music and sound effects added to give a professional and authentic feel. Production values, however, are just 'window dressing', they should never intrude or be seen as a substitute for your performance. It's your vocal qualities everyone wants to hear.

When you arrive in the studio and begin recording, you may find there's a script that's not coming together or simply doesn't feel right. If this is the case then abandon it and move on to another. You should be aiming for a 'natural' read, so never force a performance as it will always be apparent to the listener.

It's not unusual for a client to ask you to read their script in the style of something they've heard on your showreel. So it would be a mistake to include anything that took hours to perfect and needed a great deal of editing to create a finished take. Only use natural, reasonably effortless performances which require minimal editing.

The majority of showreels you will hear on agency websites are a montage of clips. This is generally enough to give clients a broad idea of how you sound. That said, they will often want to hear an entire commercial rather than an extract. Keep this in mind when planning your session. The best approach to making a showreel is for each script to be recorded and mixed in its entirety and a montage cut together from those finished mixes. This way your agent can email individual tracks to a client if needs be.

The First Clip You Hear

Getting the sequence right for a montage is an important part of the process. It needs to have rhythm and flow, but choosing the right clip to start is essential. It will be the first sound the listener hears and will persuade them to hear more.

As we mentioned earlier, the majority of work demands a natural, authentic voice, so having the most representative example at the outset gives the listener the strongest experience of your voice. Too often inexperienced voiceovers begin their showreels with material they think everyone wants to hear, rather than their natural voice. This is a mistake.

Agents and producers we spoke to were very clear about wanting to hear a short front section without any music or sound effects. It could be a personal introduction, for example and need only be 10 - 15 seconds long.

> I still like to hear just a straight voice to start with, the plain vocal quality, without any tricks or sound effects or music.
>
> **Maxine Wiltshire – Voice Agent**

Your first showreel is likely to be the only one that will consist entirely of recordings that have never been broadcast. This is typically how most voiceovers begin their careers. Once you start working and you have collected several examples, you can arrange to edit them into your showreel, gradually changing the texture and keeping it contemporary and fresh.

How often you update your reel is a matter of personal choice. Review it on a regular basis and make any improvements you or your agent feel necessary. But, if your voice and style remain fairly constant, you may not need to make any changes.

TO SUM UP

- Spend time *listening* to showreels on agency websites to get an idea of the standard that's required.

- Always begin with the most representative example of your voice and natural accent. Consider recording a specific introduction.

- Avoid other accents unless they sound authentic.

- Save examples of characterisations and impressions for a separate reel.

- Take time to find scripts that suit your voice. Be aware of your vocal quality and age, then play to those strengths.

- Let your personality shine through.

- Remain true to yourself. For example, if you're not comfortable being funny avoid comic material.

- Pick a variety of scripts to demonstrate a contrast of pace and energy e.g. upbeat, serious, happy, straight, funny etc.

- As well as the obvious 'sales' read, also demonstrate a 'real' person read.

- Aim to be believable.

- Avoid scripts that are closely associated with a particular voice as the listener will find it hard to disassociate themselves from the original.

- Avoid topical themes or occasions, as these become dated.

- Avoid mentioning specific dates for the same reason.

- Production values, such as music and sound effects, will give the listener a sense of authenticity, but it's YOU everyone wants to hear, so make sure they don't intrude.

- Monologues, book readings and poetry are not appropriate.

- Avoid scripts that feature dialogue between voices of the same gender; it confuses the listener.

- Avoid scripts that suggest the voice is filtered in some way – for example through a phone or a p.a. system.

- Only include scripts you feel completely comfortable in performing and that you can reproduce with confidence and ease.

- Avoid excessive editing to achieve a good read.

- 60 to 90 seconds has become the accepted length for a commercial montage.

Narrative Showreels

Given the nature of long-form work, the clips in a narrative showreel should be longer; the montage can afford to last two minutes or so.

Include three or four pieces that demonstrate a variety of styles: formal, inquisitive, chatty, upbeat, etc. If you choose topics that interest you rather than those you think will impress, it will help you connect with the scripts and bring them alive.

Be sure that what you choose is appropriate to your age. Often we hear younger artists choosing topics which are more suited to a mature voice. This is a shame because there's a whole range of material aimed at different age groups.

Ask yourself...

'Is your voice likely to be chosen to describe the food shortage in Africa or the nightlife in Ibiza?'

or any shade in between. This is a fairly broad illustration, but it demonstrates the variety of work that's being produced.

There are many TV channels from which to source material, including dedicated channels such as The Discovery Networks, National Geographic, History, Crime & Punishment, Biography etc.

If you have a gift for language and find the pronunciation of complicated technical words or medical terminology straightforward, then be sure to include a sample.

Character Showreels

Every animation project is different and producers are always looking to create something unique. A showreel should aim to demonstrate enough versatility and acting ability to get you noticed and called for a casting session.

Start with a natural voice. Then give me three or four characters, but they've got to be funny, sad, lively ... slightly different things; but I want to hear the acting.

Leo Neilsen – Animation Producer

Make sure that what you're offering is original and not just a collection of famous character impersonations, however excellent they may be. An animation voiceover has to be creative. Aim to demonstrate a reasonable range of vocal styles, moods and attitudes. Remembering of course to make them larger than life, but without being too wacky or over the top; there should be an element of believability about them.

Concentrate on what you do best. It's better to have four or five very good characters on your reel rather than ten that are average. Keep the production values simple, just a few sound effects.

It would be good to show that you can do a character voice and tell a story at the same time. Something that has a little bit of exchange.

Helen Stroud – Animation Producer

If you're creative you could try writing your own material. This may be a short story, involving a number of characters that interact. If writing's not your strong point, then you could bring to life one of the many excellent, children's story books available.

> I also have a character showreel for commercials. Again the cartoon type of style, but with commercial type of scripts. I've done quite a lot of commercials over the years and they've all been animated characters. So animation can blend into the commercial world especially for children; games, toys, sweets etc.
>
> **David Holt — Voiceover**

Impressions Showreels

Impressions are a specialist area of voice work. It's a niche market. The standard has to be nothing short of excellent. Stars and celebrities invariably have very busy schedules and, while they may have agreed to appear in a commercial, they may not be available for all the research that's needed before it goes into production. So, agencies often use the voice of an impressionist to give the tests an authentic feel.

This showreel should be constructed in much the same way as an animation showreel, keeping the clips longer to allow the impressions to register.

Getting Work

Having made a showreel what next?

How will you get work?

How will you promote yourself?

A number of specialist voiceover agencies exist. They aim to build a 'list' of artists which they believe cover the requirements of the market. An agent has to know the kind of work each of their artists can and cannot do in order to promote them effectively. Advertising agencies, production companies, casting directors, producers etc, will approach an agency with a brief and the agent will make suggestions from their list.

An agency website acts as a shop window for an artist, frequently displaying a photograph, short biography and latest news alongside their showreels.

They will deal with all the business such as issuing invoices, overseeing contracts, calculating the usage and chasing payments. For this they take a percentage of an artist's fees.

Self promotion can be challenging and expensive. It requires a great deal of time, effort and determination not only to get your work heard, but also to deal with the admin. In our experience most artists prefer to have an agent to deal with the contract negotiations, business and marketing.

Many producers choose to use an agency as they have access to a wider range of talent and are often given valuable casting advice.

Finding an Agent

There's no doubt it's a crowded marketplace and most agencies are oversubscribed. It is, however, by no means a closed door, just one that may need some careful research and several persistent knocks to gain entry!

Not all agents are the same; some, for example, will only consider representing working actors. So spend time researching their websites. Study their lists to see if a particular style emerges. Notice if they already represent someone with a similar voice to yours or, if you have something to offer that's not represented on their list.

> Take your time to look at each agency and find out a bit about them. Check out their style and make the effort to see where you fit in. It'll make a difference to your first approach.

> **Laura Milne — Voice Agent**

This is where an understanding of your voice and the description we suggested you create will prove invaluable. It's always useful if you can give an agent good reasons why they might want to consider you.

> They have to be able to fill a hole in the list of clients that we have. I can't have too many people that are similar.

> **Kate Davie — Voice Agent**

If a voiceover agency appears to be associated with a theatrical agency don't assume they only represent their acting clients, they may be open to other applicants.

When you approach an agent, the tone and content of your email or letter is crucial. This could make or break the initial impact you have.

Avoid sending emails to multiple recipients, treat each agency individually. They tend to receive many submissions and it soon becomes obvious which of those applicants have studied the website and tailored their application accordingly. If you haven't considered their style, what they do as an agency and whether you'll fit in, then you will lessen your chances of being noticed.

If the website publishes a contact name then use it to make a more personal application, otherwise follow their specific instructions for submissions.

 You can find a list of voiceover agents in *Contacts*, **published by Spotlight.**

In light of your research send your showreel in the preferred format. Most agencies prefer MP3 files, but there are those who prefer CDs.

If you have your own website, avoid sending links as an alternative to sound files. It can often be time consuming to access a site and find the right file.

Give yourself the best chance and make it as easy as possible for an agent to hear you.

If you're not successful, it's unlikely you will get a more detailed explanation other than their books are full or there's too great a similarity between your voice and one of their existing artists. Both are legitimate reasons, dont feel you're being fobbed off.

The sheer volume of applicants often means they're not able to offer specific feedback about your reel.

 If you post your CD and want it returned be sure to include an addressed jiffy bag with the *correct* **postage.**

When you find an agent who offers to represent you, there will be much to discuss. Consider details such as:

- The session fees that will be charged on your behalf.
- The commission rate you're being charged (typically 15% -17.5%)
- When and how you will receive the money you've earned.
- Any personal or moral objections you may have, such as smoking, meat-eating, certain political parties or corporate companies etc.

It's also likely you will need a professional headshot and a short biography. No doubt the agency will explain their precise requirements.

TO SUM UP

- Check individual agency websites, note any specific instructions regarding submissions and specifically which audio formats are preferred.

- If an agent's name is published then be sure to use it.

- Check that what you're sending is error free.

- Include a short CV. Mention your natural accent and any experience you have, including relevant professional training.

- Avoid sending links to a website.

- If anything sent by post needs to be returned, then include an SAE with the *correct* postage.

- Be patient – you may have to wait for a response.

- Be politely persistent – but don't pester.

- Accept that getting any detailed feedback about your showreel is unlikely.

What Can You Expect to Earn?

Potential annual income could range from £500 – £100,000 or more.

That said, there are now very few artists who consider voice work as their only source of income. If you're an actor, then it can be a valuable part of your working life. If you're not an actor, then it's unlikely to be your only career.

PART FIVE
VOICE AND BODY

PART FIVE – VOICE AND BODY

For much voiceover work you'll be sitting in front of a microphone and this in itself presents an issue to be taken into account.

Posture and Breath

Posture

Your posture affects your voice. So here are a few basic exercises.

 Often when seated we tend to collapse in the middle so that the muscles around the waist and lower abdomen are slumped. This will have a negative effect on your breathing and therefore on the sound you make.

- Start this exercise by deliberately sitting in a slumped way. Notice how you feel when the breath comes and goes, read a paragraph or two out loud from a newspaper or magazine.

- Imagine that you're a puppet and that you have a wire attached to the crown of your head and the puppeteer is gently pulling up on it. This will give you a sense of lift through the length of the spine and particularly through the back of the neck. You're aiming for a sense of upward moving energy from the tailbone to the crown of the head, but at the same time, a feeling of softness through the breastbone and on down through the solar plexus and abdominal muscles.

- Place your feet on the floor as if you were standing, that is, within the margins of your hip sockets. Lift one knee at a time so that your foot comes off the floor, flex, rotate and shake the foot and replace.

- Now consciously relax your buttock muscles.

- Next check your shoulders are relaxed and sitting softly in place. Roll your shoulder blades back and forth (like shrugging off and on a coat.) Bounce your shoulder blades up and down a few times.

- Let the jaw relax, so the lips fall open, make sure there's a little space between the back teeth.

- Induce a yawn – aim to make it as wide as you can and not just vertical.

- Stretch and release your tongue a couple of times. Gently connect the front of your tongue behind your lower front teeth where they emerge from the gums. Stretch the middle of your tongue forward and release like a wave over your bottom lip. Repeat several times then encourage your tongue to lie in the bottom of your mouth.

- Encourage your breath to come in over the lips and imagine it dropping down through the centre of your body, as if it could sink right down to the space between your hip sockets. Once again read a couple of paragraphs from a newspaper or magazine. Notice the difference from when you did this in the slumped position.

Your posture is also affected by physical tension, particularly in long sessions, and most commonly focuses in the back of the neck and shoulders. The muscles in your throat, around your larynx, can also become tense, which affects your voice. The above exercises will also help with this issue.

A lot of voice artists have neck and back problems because the tension has to go somewhere.

Teresa Gallagher – Voiceover

Approaching the Microphone

Developing, what is for you, a comfortable relationship with the microphone is important, especially when the sound engineer comes to adjust it in a session.

To help achieve this you can practise at home.

- Imagine a microphone in front of you, use a lamp; (one of the angled desk lamps is perfect.) As you speak, don't allow your chin to jut forward as this throws the larynx out of alignment and puts extra pressure on the delicate mechanism. You may survive for short periods, but if you are working on a lengthy script your voice will become tired and strained. Over time this type of vocal posture may even cause damage.

- With one hand cupped behind an ear to give some feedback, practise your approach to the mic: closer for the warmer, more intimate reads, slightly further away for those requiring higher energy. Throughout a recording it's important to maintain your optimum physical position.

- As you practise, aim for a sense of inner relaxation. Releasing a couple of 'deep sighs of relief' without voice will help you do this.

- You can increase the effectiveness of your practice by recording and playing back as described earlier in the book.

Breath

Much of the voiceover work you'll be doing, will require you to deliver a script with a sense of flow. Noisy breath sounds will be impossible to edit out of the recording. If there's tension around the way you breathe or if you habitually snatch breaths, it will immediately become apparent.

- Sit quietly, but in the good posture position and without thinking about it too much, breathe as you would normally.

- Place a hand on the upper chest. Does this area move up and down as the breath comes and goes?

- Next, place both hands on the lower part of the rib-cage at the sides. Is there movement here?

- Now gently place a hand on the space just above your navel. What sort of movement is happening here?

- Finally, check how the breath is entering your body. Is it through your nose or mouth?

- Recall, or consciously check, how your breath comes and goes in a dialogue with someone else. Of course it'll be affected by the emotional temperature of the interaction, but basically you'll notice that the breath enters your body over the lips and lasts for as long as the thought you want to express. You'll notice you 're-fuel' as necessary depending on what you have to say. Rarely do you breathe through your nose between thoughts, and if you do, it may be a sign that you're trying to keep your temper or giving yourself extra time to put a check on the flow of what you are saying.

- Bearing this in mind, lick your lips to help you feel the cool air coming in, sense it dropping to a central place on a level with the bottom edge of your rib cage. The warm, outgoing breath immediately bounces back and then there's a moment of stillness before the next cool 'in' breath happens. Spend a few minutes to allow this natural rhythm to establish.

- To activate your breath try the 'sigh of relief'. First, yawn your throat open, then imagine you've been waiting for some good news, you have almost given up on it, but then it finally comes and you give a HUGE sigh of relief, on breath only, no voice. Recreate this thought and huge sigh of relief four times. Try not to let your shoulders and upper chest 'heave' upwards as the breath comes in. Aim for a sense of your breath sinking low into the body.

- Next imagine a scenario that would provoke a smaller or medium sigh of relief and repeat this six times. Once again, focus on the breath dropping.

- Finally, create many, many excited, anticipatory panting breaths (like a puppy about to be taken for a walk); 10-15 at a time, with a short rest in between. Be sure to allow the panting breaths to come and go over the lips rather than pumping out one breath using your stomach muscles. If you feel your breath catching on your throat, yawn once more.

- Throughout, allow your stomach and buttock muscles to be relaxed. If you're released in this way, your breath will respond to the intensity, length and feeling of the thoughts you're going to express.

- Now, return to reading out loud. If you can increase the length and difficulty of the text while staying in this optimum position for posture, relaxation and breath.

Of course in a voiceover session you'll become engaged with the script and your posture and breath may change but, by practising at home and then reminding yourself between takes, the ideal will become second nature.

A Vocal Warm-Up

 It's important to keep your voice healthy and flexible. Here's a short vocal warm-up which you should aim to do three times a week, whether you are working or not and always before a job.

Take a couple of minutes to stretch out in whichever way you feel your body needs. Yawn as you stretch. Give yourself a general shake out, like a dog getting out of a pond.

- Roll your shoulder-blades back and let them drop into place, like shrugging off a coat. Do the reverse, like shrugging on a coat. Repeat several times.

- Massage the base of your neck and either side of the vertebrae in your neck, up towards the rim of the skull.

- Float your elbows up to shoulder height, then float up your wrists and finally let your fingers float up towards the ceiling. Next stretch upwards letting the impetus come from the lower back ribs rather than the top of the shoulders.

- Release the stretch by allowing the shoulder blades to slide down on a small outward breath ... **fff**. Repeat.

- Next release just your fingers on a small outward **fff** breath, followed by the wrists …**fff**, the elbows …**fff** then let your head fall forward …**fff**. Let the weight of your head provide the impetus for rolling down towards the floor on a long outward **fff** until you are 'hanging' from the waist. Try not to brace the knees but encourage a sense of softness behind them, soften your stomach muscles, ease out your shoulders and gently nod your head. Roll back up vertebra by vertebra starting at the tail-bone, let you shoulders fall into place before (this is very important) building up the vertebrae in your neck to bring your head back up on top of your shoulders.

Breath

- Stretch up on one side and yawn in the breath through your mouth to the ribs on that side and release on an outward sigh … no sound. Repeat on the other side.
- Give yourself a hug, let your head drop forward rounding the back and yawn the breath in through the mouth to the back ribs and release on a sigh … no sound. Let your arms float out to the side, arch your spine, head back, bend your knees slightly opening up your front ribs and yawn the breath in and release on a sigh … no sound. Come back to an upright position.
- Roll down once more, let the breath in and sigh out from your tailbone, this time with sound … huhhh! Roll up on a long outward **sssss** breath, remembering to let the shoulders fall into place before letting the head come up.

Humming

- Massage your face moving the skin and muscle. Let your hands rest lightly on your face. Sigh a **HUM** onto your lips.
- Continue humming. Move up and down in pitch encouraging the sense of the sound radiating out from your lips through the bones of your face and skull. Let the **hum** fall from the top of your skull, down your face like a waterfall and release into **uhhhh** (as in the middle of 'her') as you tap the bones of your upper chest with lightly clenched fists.

Developing Sound

- Raise an arm, slap or squeeze the muscles up and down then sigh a hum as you shake and loosen the muscles releasing into an **uhhhh** sound as if shaking the sound from your finger ends … **hummmmuhhh**! Repeat with the other arm.
- Roll and shake your shoulder-blades … **hummmmmuhhhh**!
- Take a moderately wide stance and circle your pelvic region, flutter your lips **brrrrmmmm**. Then sigh **brrrrmmmmmmuhhh**! Repeat a few times circling in different directions. and moving up and down in pitch.

- Slap and squeeze down the muscles of each leg then hum into sound (**hummmmuhhh**) shaking as you did with your arms.
- Throw an imaginary ball to various points on **hummmmuhhh** going down and up on pitches.

Opening Spaces in the Mouth and Throat

- With the heel of your hands gently massage around the hinge of your jaw and then draw your jaw down with your hands in an up, forward and back motion while releasing an outward sigh. Take hold of your chin between thumbs and forefingers, elbows out to the side, and manually open and close your jaw taking care not to clash your teeth. Sigh out on breath as you do this, feeling the breath travelling up and over the hard palate. Release your hands.
- Yawn your breath in and bring the back of your tongue up to the soft palate, releasing a **gah gah** sound as you reach out or up. Hold an imaginary bow and arrow. As you draw the arrow back make an **ng** sound and as you release the arrow let the sound turn into **ahhh**. Repeat to different focus points allowing the throat to be open on the outgoing sound.
- Lightly connect the front of your tongue behind your lower front teeth where they come out of the gum. Stretch the back of your tongue forward like a wave over the bottom lip and release. Repeat several times sighing as you go.
- Then with less of a forward stretch, as if shaking the middle of your tongue, repeat on a sighing **huhyuhyuhyuhyuh**.

Resonance

Place a couple of fingers into the curve of your neck, let your head come back, let your jaw release, open your throat and imagine a wide open space from your lips down to your pelvic floor. A little like a chimney, wide at the bottom and narrow at the top. Sigh up from the bottom low in your range **Hahhh**. Then, **hahh hahh hahh hahh**. Let your neck lengthen so that your skull comes up on top, sigh through the roof of your mouth on a mid range, **Huhhh**. Then, **huhh huhh huhh huhh**. Lengthen your neck once more so that your skull comes forward, chin towards your chest, sigh in the upper range into the top teeth on **Heeee**. Then, **hee hee hee hee**. Reverse the process. Come back to head on top of shoulders. Repeating long **hey** sounds lightly beat your upper chest, swing your arms. Call out as if to a friend across the street ... **Hey**!

There is more than one way to hum. The most effective in a warm-up gives you a 'buzz' on the lips. This requires space between your teeth at the back of the mouth and for your tongue to be soft in the bottom of your mouth. If your tongue is raised at the front or at the back it will send the sound into the nose, which is not what you are aiming for.

Articulation

 As if juggling or tapping a tom-tom drum, play with the sounds … **buh/duh/buh/ duh/buh/duh** … **duh/buh/duh/buh/duh/buh** etc. Move on to … **guh/duh/guh/ duh/guh/duh** and **duh/guh/duh/guh/duh/guh** etc. Combine **buh/duh/guh/duh** and **duh/guh/buh/duh**.

Whisper: **puh/tuh/puh/tuh/puh/tuh** and **tuh/kuh/tuh/kuh/tuh/kuh** and **kuh/tuh/kuh/tuh/ kuh/tuh**.

Combine into: **puh/tuh/kuh/tuh** and **kuh/tuh/puh/tuh**.

Spring **w**'s off the lips … **will you, will you, will you. Will you wait? Why? When? What? Where?**

Add some tongue twisters if you like and finish with some text.

If you want to do more in depth work on your voice we recommend *Freeing the Natural Voice* by Kristin Linklater.

Vowels and Consonants

It's been said that the greater part of the body can contribute to the sound of the voice. As you explore your voice, be open to the possibility that different sounds in words can inhabit different spaces in your body.

The vowel sound **oo**, for example, wants to sit down in the pelvic area, the sound **ee** in the top of the head. In between, **aw** sits around the solar plexus, **ah** across the upper chest and **er** in the roof of the mouth.

Additionally, consonant sounds have distinct qualities. Notice, for example, how **buh**, **duh** and **guh**, are made with voiced sounds and **puh**, **tuh**, and **kuh**, are made with air alone. Feel this difference by speaking the first set and whispering the second. Try out the vibrancy of **zzz** and the silkiness of **sss**, the tingle of **vvv** and the mistiness of **fff**.

If you develop an awareness of where these sounds sit in the mouth and how they combine with vowels you'll begin to get the feeling that voice and speech are part of your body.

For an exploration of how vowels and consonants can be embodied there is an excellent chapter on the subject in Kristin Linklater's book *Freeing Shakespeare's Voice*.

Sight-Reading Exercise

To help increase the fluency of your sight-reading, you can also try exercises used by voice coaches to unlock text. The following is derived from Cicely Berry's work.

- Take a piece of advertising copy, a section of an instruction manual or transcribe a segment of narration from a documentary programme.

- If you have a garden or live near an open space 'walk the punctuation'. This involves first walking to the full stops, question marks and exclamation points. Make your walk purposeful and when you come to one of these punctuation marks STOP, make a 90 degree turn and walk on to the next. This will reveal to you the basic sentence/thought structure of the piece.

- Next check if there are any semi-colons or colons. These are the points where the sentence or thought might have ended, but in fact it continues, often in an interesting way. Walk the text once more adding in these 'turning' points. Check how this has informed your understanding of the structure of the piece.

- You can go on to walk the text once more, adding in all the commas. This may help you get the structure and rhythm of the piece into your body and breath. Do remember, however, that commas often serve a grammatical purpose, such as either side of a name, and do not necessarily indicate a pause or a breathing point. If, however, you do use a comma as a small breath point make sure that you are not breaking up the sense of the thought.

If the idea of doing this exercise in a public space deters you, then you can alter it, by using two chairs in the privacy of your home. Place the chairs a little way apart.

Using the punctuation in exactly the same way as above start with full stops, question marks and exclamation points. As you say the first word of the sentence drop down into a chair, let the action bounce the word out of you. Continue to the next 'big' punctuation mark and then move to the other chair for the start of the next sentence. Don't speak in mid-air and work your way through the piece as before.

Here are a couple of very useful exercises developed by Barbara Houseman:

Phrase by Phrase. Use an object or photograph of a person to focus your attention, as if you are speaking to someone. Using the piece of copy take the first phrase, that is, up to the first punctuation point, take in what it's saying then look up to the object/photograph and speak it out loud. Go through the whole piece in this way, then read the whole out loud, looking up as often as you can to keep your focus on speaking to one person.

Practise in front of a mirror. That way you will realise how often you lift your eyes off the page to engage with your audience. When reading in front of a mirror, your audience is your own reflection. When reading in front of a mic, the mic itself becomes your audience. If you haven't caught your own eye in the mirror very often, this means you are focusing too much on the page and need to lift the reading up off the page more. You are story—TELLING, and you must include your listeners.

Tamsin Collinson — Audiobook Director

Gather together seven objects of different weights and sizes. Begin to read through a piece of text and as you come across a word or phrase that you think shifts the thought, pick up an object, look up from the page to a lamp, chair or some other focus point and as you say the word or phrase 'show' the object to whatever it is you are focusing on.

Example: 'The boy – OBJECT – stood – OBJECT – on the burning – OBJECT – deck – OBJECT ...'

Work through the whole piece, but don't over-think the exercise. Rely instead on your instincts. If you repeat this exercise with the same piece of text you will probably find additional ways in which the thought shifts. Then speak the text through normally.

Over time these exercises will sharpen up your response to text enabling you to deliver a piece of sight-reading with fluency and depth.

Looking After Your Voice

Voiceover work is demanding and you'll need to take care of your voice.

> *Most artists I've known who have had vocal problems have got over them by looking after their voices properly.*

> **Teresa Gallagher – Voiceover**

Voice strain and loss is often directly related to misuse. For example, shouting, screaming, speaking against a noisy background, 'vocally pushing' and habitual throat clearing.

Throat Clearing

When you clear your throat, the vocal cords rub tightly together as outgoing air passes between them. This causes irritation of the vocal folds and they then produce more mucous to protect themselves. The presence of this mucous makes you want to clear your throat again to get rid of it, aggravating the problem. Instead of throat clearing, sip water or do a hard swallow.

A Sore Throat

We all get sore throats from time to time. When this happens rest your voice as much as possible and avoid unnecessary use. If you need to speak, do so quietly, but don't whisper. Avoid medicated throat lozenges and instead suck pastilles, those containing glycerine are particularly soothing. Honey can also be comforting.

Keep hydrated but avoid drinks that are very hot or very cold. Steam inhalations can also relieve soreness.

Irritants

Many of us have allergies or sensitivities to certain foods or dust, dust mite and pollen. If this is the case, pay attention to your diet and seek out suitable treatments.

Many irritants will cause the mucous membranes of the throat to be irritated. Here are some common examples:

- Speaking against a background of noise can cause you to push your voice which results in strain.

- Alcohol – heavy use (3+ units per day) can result in a husky, rough, low-pitched voice. Spirits are a particular irritant as they dry out the mucus membranes of the larynx.

- Smoking – avoid all types of smoking as it has a profound drying effect on the throat and surrounding areas. The tars and irritants in the smoke cause irritation of the mucus air passage linings and this can adversely affect voice quality. Unfortunately, passive smoking can have the same effects.

- Dust, fumes, chemicals – can irritate the tissues in the throat.

- Heating systems and air-conditioning dry out the throat.

- Hot drinks and hot, spicy foods cause dehydration and remove mucus from the throat.

TO SUM UP

- Drink plenty of water (room temperature is ideal) especially when you're working.

- Pay attention to how you use your voice, aim to produce a free and flexible voice.

- Ensure that there are times during the day when you can rest your voice.

- Take time to relax and unwind.

- Instead of throat clearing, sip water or do a hard swallow.

Dyslexia

We should start by saying that dyslexia is not necessarily an impediment to voice work. However, it has to be managed realistically. The first thing to say is that dyslexia doesn't define you, it defines an aspect of your processing. The signs and symptoms vary with each individual.

Broadly there are three principles on which the classification of dyslexia rests:

- **Persistent literary difficulties**: that is a history of difficulty in acquiring language skills. Reading, writing and spelling may not all have been affected, but one of these aspects of literacy will have caused problems.
- **Short-term memory** may be impaired.
- **Processing speed**: that is the ability to take in information, absorb it and repeat it. For example, by answering questions, writing an essay or speaking it out loud.

Should I be tested?

This will depend on the degree to which you feel that whenever you commit your thought processes to the written word you have difficulty in expressing what you think you know about the text.

If you decide to have a diagnosis made, it's crucial that a qualified, accredited assessor tests you. Organisations such as The British Dyslexia Association (bdadyslexia.org.uk) and Dyslexia Action (dyslexiaaction.org.uk) will be able to point you in the right direction.

It's beyond the scope of this book to develop, in any depth, strategies to deal with this issue. Following diagnosis though, you may be offered specialist help.

That said, if you experience difficulties then practise will help.

Here are some useful tips.

- When reading out loud use a finger to direct your gaze along the lines, therefore stopping you from skipping down. This will also help you follow the sentences to the full stops and prevent you from energetically ending a thought at other punctuation before the sense of the line is complete.
- It may also help to 'chunk' the text. Use a small card, to block out some of the text so that your eye cannot skip down.

For some people the contrast between a white page and the black ink can cause an issue. Coloured 'overlays' are available which calm the contrast between the two.

Stress can exacerbate the difficulties. Mindfulness practice will help and some have found neurolinguistic programming (NLP) beneficial. Certainly, before a recording session, releasing physical tensions and focussing on your breath will help manage stress.

It's well worth trying the sight-reading exercises earlier in the book.

Finally, you should of course let your agent know, but other than that there's no need to wear it on a T-shirt!

AND ...

AND ...

Other Crumbs of Advice

Throughout the book we have included some valuable advice from agents, producers, engineers and voiceovers. Here are some of the other crumbs of advice they offered:

Agents

Get some acting experience. Go to drama school and tread the boards for as long as you can.

Sue Terry – Voice Agent, Sue Terry Voices

Have good manners and respect for the people you're working for. Go in with the right attitude and when you're being directed listen to what they're saying to you.

They're paying you and they want it the way that they want it. It's not down to you to tell them how it should be.

Helen Gallwey – Voice Agent, Yakety Yak

Always be on time,

Always be polite,

Always do as you're asked.

Helen Gallwey – Voice Agent, Yakety Yak

Don't think you can make a living out of voiceover work. If you want to be an actor, it should be another string to your bow.

Martin Sims – Voice Agent, Earache Voices

I would use my smartphone an awful lot and record into it, and listen to it and really, really think about what your USP is and whether you're going to be good for this market, before you spend a penny going out to a studio.

Maxine Wiltshire – Voice Agent, Voice Shop

Artists

Don't try and do everything. Do what you can do, because people will hire you for you.

Be an adaptable version of yourself – be your own voice, but be able to take direction.

Bethan James – Voiceover

I always depend on my engineer - they are all hugely skilled. Listen to what they say; work with him/her and between you (and often <u>despite</u> the client) you will deliver magic.

Miriam Margolyes – Voiceover

Have a chat at the beginning but not too long, just enough to relax them. Remember, if you're nervous they're equally concerned that they've chosen the right voice.

Sue Elliott-Nicholls – Voiceover

Do what the director wants even if your head is spinning with ideas. The director has booked you because they too have a vision. Once you've done what they've asked you to do and they're happy, then offer your suggestions.

Sue Elliott-Nicholls – Voiceover

Know what your own voice is. Be easy to work with.

Christopher Kent – Voiceover

To get started using a variety of accents and impressions, I would suggest listening to the radio and TV ads and recording as many as you can. By doing your 'homework' you'll get used to the styles of 'reads' and become more confident at sight-reading.

Script some of the ads you enjoy and then practise reading them aloud and recording them. Work on the timings and pace of the ads. The more you practise, the more confident you'll become.

Caroline Bernstein – Voiceover and Impressionist

Do your preparation so you feel as confident as possible before you step into the room. Because you're not going to see the script beforehand it's about you knowing that you feel comfortable with sight-reading a script and making the best of the material you've been given. And enjoy it as much as possible.

Nico Lennon – Voiceover

Whether you think that you can, or that you can't, you're usually right. Self-belief, confidence and persistence are absolutely vital to success. Be honest with yourself: if you're not good at something, practise and get feedback. It's so obvious, but I'm always amazed at how few people do it.

Deidre Mullins – Voiceover / Continuity Presenter
quoting Henry Ford

The requirements are as much PREPARATION as possible, the STAMINA and CONCENTRATION to spend days in a studio and perhaps most importantly try and ENJOY the experience. That way the listener will benefit from the actor's positive input.

Christian Rodska – Voiceover

I always view the voice work for animation as an acting job not a voiceover job. It requires acting skills – you've got to create a character out of thin air. You are creating an audio voice track from which the animators get lots of ideas, they get inspired if it's a really good voice track. So the more acting you can get into it the better. It has to be truthful and true to the character, however wild and crazy the situation is.

The character is the star, not you. It's a collaborative process between yourself, as the voice that's creating the character vocally and the animator creating the character visually. If the two work well together then the character is believable. The children watching don't care who the voice is, what matters to them is whether it's believable.

David Holt –Voiceover

'Just remember that no-one can see you!' That, for me, encapsulates the need to express everything in your voice, the freedom and lack of stereotype that voice work affords you and the lack of ego which prevails amongst many voiceovers.

Eve Karpf – Voiceover

Producers

Ask questions. Don't keep doing something over and over again without finding out why. Say something like 'OK great but was there something you didn't like in the last read, something I can do better?'

Ask questions because you may draw something out of them they don't know how to express.

Ben Fairman – Producer

Always have a section on your showreel where it's actually you. Something that sounds like you in your own natural range.

Pam Myers – Producer

Having a good connection with the producer is important. Some voiceovers make an assumption as to what is needed; it's always best to have a discussion first.

Some producers may also assume you know what you're doing.

Max McGonigal – MD Crow TV

Relax, be yourself. Listen to the direction and take your time. Even if it comes out way too long, get the shape and sound first, then you can always quicken it.

Paul Burke – Producer

You're selling an hour of your time to a producer ... leave all other thoughts, considerations and distractions outside.

Christopher Kent – Producer

I've heard rumours of voiceovers who are also bikers turning up in their leathers, then realising they are squeaking and having to stand there in their underpants! So dress appropriately.

Helen Stroud – Producer

When you're doing a voice for animation you have to exaggerate otherwise it doesn't work in cartoon form.

Leo Neilsen – Producer

Some actors are a little bit reticent about taking direction. Most of what we do is subjective. It might be the director's interpretation of how a line should be delivered and they may not see it that way. Ultimately though where does the buck stop?

Some people have it innately, they just get it. It's practice and understanding of how it works. Being able to do a lot of things, having a lot of things going on in your mind.

Tony Church – Producer

Sound Engineers

It doesn't matter who you are, don't be late. Especially if you've another session straight after at another studio. You'll feel stressed and I think it goes against you. Timekeeping is important.

Be mindful of over-criticising the script. Clients will tolerate the odd suggestion, but remember it has been through a fairly rigorous process before it reaches the studio. So be respectful at all times.

Be pleasant, be nice to the engineer because they can help you out in all sorts of ways, they're the person that maybe saves you at the end of the day.

Chris Southwell – Sound Engineer

Tune your ear so that you truly understand what's needed.

Nick Angell – Sound Engineer/Voice Director

Don't turn up to a session hungry!

Tim Lofts – Sound Engineer

[Referring to animation.] If you're just starting out working in an ensemble, great, because you can see how these other more experienced people are doing it and you can learn from that.

I learnt the most about my job when I was starting out as an assistant engineer and was watching someone do the job I aspired to.

Be prepared. We all have to prepare, and if you arrive having an understanding of the script, that's a great start.

Nick Harris — Sound Engineer/Voice Director

In a Nutshell ...

A voiceover is a professional performer

Know your own voice and the way others hear you

Let your vocal personality shine through

Know your strengths

A feeling for language and the way words work is invaluable

Improve your sight-reading – read aloud EVERY day

Acting skills *will* be helpful

Believe in what you're saying, for the time you're saying it

Clarity, irrespective of accent or vocal quality, is vital.

Always be 'In the Moment'

Listen, *really* listen

Develop a sense of timing

Aim for a one-to-one performance

The more you practise the better you'll become

Never be late

Work *with* your clients to make a creative relationship

Avoid being negative about the script

Develop your internal director

If you're not sure, ASK!

Take care of your voice

And oh yes...

don't eat toast ... at least not in a session!

Terminology

Every industry has its terminology

Agent   Person that acts for and promotes an artist.

Agency   Company that acts for and promotes a list of artists.

Animatic   Simple video to test an idea for a commercial.

Bande Rythmo   Rythmo Band. French technique used in dubbing.

Brief   A document given to an advertising agency by the company that needs a product or service advertised.

Cans   Headphones.

Casting Session An opportunity for the production team to hear various artists interpret and perform a part of their script.

Client   Ultimately the person or company who has commissioned the project is known as 'The Client'. In this context, however, it is also the person or company who booked the voiceover.

Commercial Sectors Recognised areas of advertising:
Broadband, Business & Industrial, Car Parking, Clothing & Accessories, Comparison Websites, Computers, Cosmetics & Toiletries, Drink, DVD Rental, Entertainment & The Media, Environment Issues, Finance, Food, Gardening & Agriculture, Government/Political/Social, Health, Household, Internet, Leisure equipment, Mail Order, Motors, Office, Online Dating, Online shopping, Pharmaceutical, Property, Recruitment, Recycling, Retail, Satnavs, Telecoms, Tobacco, Travel & Transport, Utilities.

Continuity Announcer The voice heard between TV or radio programmes.

Control Room Where the technical and creative aspects of the session are controlled.

Copy   Written material in a number of contexts, notably advertising and publishing.

Copywriter   Person who writers the script or 'copy'.

Creative Team Generally a copywriter and an art director. Together they work as a team in the creative department of an advertising agency where the campaign is created. They're often referred to as 'the creatives'.

Cue   Indication by hand, light or voice, to begin speaking.

Drop-in   An insert into a previously recorded section;
'We're just going to drop you in for that one line.'

(Sound) Engineer	Person responsible for the recording, editing and mixing of the sound.
Facility	Term used for companies providing one or more specific audio or visual services to the industry.
Fluff	A mistake or stumble when reading.
FVO	Female Voiceover.
Guide track	Often spoken by the editor or producer, it is used to time sequences of video that will eventually be spoken by a voiceover.
Hard-sell	A commercial that uses a direct, forceful and overt sales message. see also *Soft Sell*
Headshot	Portrait photograph – head and shoulders – used for publicity purposes.
ISDN	Acronym: Integrated Services Digital Network. A high quality, digital telephone line. It enables studios and end users to exchange digital data around the world in real time. It's relatively cheap to set up and became very popular with many voiceovers who felt they could work from home. Particularly popular in the USA.
Level	The volume of sound.
Lift	A copy. *'We'll send you a 'lift' of that commercial.'*
Long-form	More than two pages of script. Generally narration for documentary or corporate work.
Lip-Sync	Matching lip movement with spoken word.
Mic	Widely used abbreviation for 'Microphone'.
Microphone	Key component in the recording process. Most studios use high-quality condenser microphones.
TV Monitor	High-quality TV screen.
MVO	Male Voiceover.
Pencil	A provisional booking.
Pick-up	Re-record a specific line or section of the script.
A Pitch	Selling an idea to a prospective client. Advertising agencies will 'pitch' to a company in order to secure their business.
Playback	To hear what's been recorded.
Pop	Sound created by a forceful consonant such as P, T and K arriving on a sensitive microphone and causing a break-up of the signal.
Pop shields	Deflects plosive consonants away from the highly sensitive microphone.

Post Production	A variety of processes needed to create a final production ready for transmission or distribution. Includes voiceover recording, editing, adding music, sound effects and mixing etc.
Producers and PAs	A TV producer sources directors and production companies, negotiates budgets and manages the shoots/ recordings. Producers normally start as a PA (Production Assistant) working closely with the TV producers, learning the skills and shadowing them on shoots and recordings.
Product Area	see *Commercial Sectors*
Promo	see *Trailers*
Recording Booth	see *Voice Booth*
Recording Studio	see *Sound Studio*
Representation	An agent is known to represent an artist.
Re-versioning	The process of making an English spoken version of a documentary, animation or commercial.
Rock 'n' Roll	Old term for dropping in as the recording session progresses.
RP	Received Pronunciation. A standard, southern-English accent.
Session	A period of pre-booked time in a studio.
Soft-sell	A commercial that uses a subtle, casual, or friendly sales message. see also *Hard Sell*
SFX	Abbreviation for Sound Effects.
Short-form	A short script of no more than two pages; generally commercials, trailers or announcements.
Showreel	Collection of clips, often in the form of a montage, to demonstrate vocal qualities, sometime referred to as a voicereel.
Sound Studio	Soundproofed rooms where sound recordings are made.
Sync Sound	Refers to the words of contributors/experts/actors/ public etc. seen speaking in a film.
Take	A 'take' is the name given to a piece of text or an action that has been recorded. Each time the same piece is recorded it is given a different take number; take one, take two etc.
Talkback	Simply a communications device to enable those in the control room to talk to the studio or voice booth.
Tease	In a factual programme/documentary the section of narration before the TITLE sequence can be referred to as the TEASE.
Time-code	Displayed as HOURS: MINUTES: SECONDS: FRAMES; it is used to visually navigate a video.

To Picture	Working with the video as a visual reference. 'We will be working to picture.'
Toast	A slice of bread, browned by exposure to radiant heat that should NEVER be eaten during a session!
Trailer	Short advert announcement of a forthcoming TV programme or feature film.
TV Department	Within the TV Department of an advertising agency there will often be a Head of TV, TV Producers and Production Assistants (PAs). The department is responsible for the production of all TV and radio commercials, cinema advertising etc.
	see also *Producers and PAs*
VO	abbreviation for 'Voiceover'.
Voice Booth	Soundproofed and isolated room where an artist's performance is recorded.
Voice Reel	see *Showreel*
Vox pop	Short for *vox populi*, meaning voice of the people. 'People on the street' interviews are often referred to as 'Vox Pops'.
Walla	Specifically used in animation, this a library of human sound: oohs, ahs, grunts, groans, screams, laughs etc. These may be individual or as a crowd. Generally improvised in the studio.
Wild	When there's neither a picture or other sound to influence the voice recording.
Wild lines	Specific lines or ad-libs recorded separately from the rest of the script.
Wind shields	Sculptured foam rubber that fits over the microphone and protects the diaphragm from wind and condensation.

Further Reading

Berry, Cicely, *Text In Action* (Virgin Publishing, 2001)

Berry, Cicely, *The Actor and The Text* (Virgin Books, 2000)

Houseman, Barbara, *Tackling Text [and subtext]: A Step-by-Step Guide for Actors* (Nick Hern Books, 2008)

Karpf, Anne, *The Human Voice: The Story of a Remarkable Talent* (Bloomsbury Publishing, 2006)

Linklater, Kristin, *Freeing the Natural Voice* (Nick Hern Books, 2006)

Linklater, Kristin, *Freeing Shakespeare's Voice* (Nick Hern Books, 2010)

Our Thanks ...

We have to thank our contributors for their time, insights and generosity.

First then, those that helped with reading, correcting and commenting on our words: Deidre Mullins (who was sensitive enough to only be constructive about our first draft), Hattie Eastcott, Bethan James, Sue Elliott-Nicholls. And of course, Melina Theocharidou, our supportive editor at Oberon.

A special thank you to Helen Stroud at Collingwood & Co who arranged for us to reproduce the sides and character breakdown in Animation and made the connections with Tony Church, David Holt and Nick Harris.

Of course the legendary Miriam, she of many, many voices, who didn't hesitate for a second when we asked if she'd write the Foreword. Then our interviewees, some of whom wear more than one hat in our industry, who gave us the insights and advice to pass on:

Voice agents:

Helen Gallwey, Yakety Yak

Jane Savage, Calypso Voices

Johnny Garcia, Rhubarb Voices

Kate Davie, Head of United Voices

Laura Milne, The Joneses Voiceover Agency

Martin Sims, owner of Earache Voices

Maxine Wiltshire, owner of Voice Shop

Sue Terry, owner of Sue Terry Voices

Producers:

Ben Fairman, Radioville

Christopher Kent, owner of CKUK Media

Helen Stroud, Head of Development at Collingwood & Co

Leo Neilsen, owner of King Rollo Films

Martin Sims, owner of Eardrum

Max McGonigal, MD at Crow TV

Pam Myers, owner of Rorschach

Paul Burke, owner of Paul Burke Radio

Tamsin Collinson, Audiobooks Director

Tony Church, owner of Tony Church Projects

Sound Engineers:

Chris Southwell, UNIT Post Production Services

Dave Peacock, voice director, owner of Peacock Sound

Nick Angell, voice director, owner of Angell Sound Studios

Nick Harris, voice director, owner of Tamborine Productions

Tim Lofts, owner of On Air Sound Design

Voice Artists:

Ben Fairman

Bethan James

Bob Golding

Caroline Bernstein

Christian Rodska

Christopher Kent

David Holt

Deidre Mullins

Elizabeth Conboy

Eve Karpf

Martin Sims

Nico Lennon

Sue Elliott-Nicholls

Teresa Gallagher

Miriam Margolyes

Specialists:

Chris Bailey, vocal health advice

Tanya Zybutz, expert dyslexia guidance

Audio/Visual Resource Pack File Listing

Open your internet browser and go to
www.oberonbooks.com/voiceover

1. Click the download link in the middle of the page.

2. A compressed zip file (TheVoiceOverBook.zip) will automatically begin downloading.

3. Once it has finished, go to the designated download folder on your computer.

4. Right click on TheVoiceOverBook.zip, and click 'Extract'.

5. When prompted enter the password: **TVOB521**

6. This will open a folder named 'The VoiceOver Book Resource Pack', containing the media files.

7. Simply drag and drop or copy and paste these files to wherever you wish to store them on your computer.

8. If you require any further technical support, please contact **info@oberonbooks.com** or telephone **+44 (0)207 607 3637**.

	PAGE	TITLE	TYPE	DESCRIPTION
A1	16	Flat Speech / Engaging Speech	A	Example of dull flat speech and engaging speech.
A2	29	The First Word and the Last	A	Example of a cold start and tailing off at the end.
A3	52	Working with a Guide Track	A and PDF	A pdf script and guide track for practice.
A4	61	Snatched Breath and Over-modulated Pick-up	A	Example and how to resolve this issue.
A5	87	Articulation	A	
V1	49	Microphone Technique	V	How close you should be to the mic, proximity effect, being off mic.
V2	49	Pops (and Sibilance)	V	Demonstration of hand in front of mouth, single finger, turn head, angle mic at 45° and pop shield.
V3	51	Wearing Headphones	V	One on, one off.
V4	80	Posture and Breath	V	A demonstration.
V5	82	Approaching the Mic	V	A demonstration.
V6	84	Simple Stretches for Vocal Warm-up	V	A demonstration.
V7	85	Breath	V	A demonstration.
V8	86	Resonance	V	A demonstration.

NOTES